I0802745

Fred Cockerham & Tommy Jarrell Clawhammer Banjo Masters

Clawhammer Banjo Tablature as Played by Fred and Tommy with modern interpretations by Bob Carlin and Dan Levenson

Online Audio

1 As Time Draws Near - Bob
2 As Time Draws Near- Dan
3 Back Step Cindy - Bob
4 Back Step Cindy - Dan
5 Big Eyed Rabbit - Bob
6 Big Eyed Rabbit - Dan
7 Ducks on The Millpond - Bob
8 Ducks on The Millpond - Dan
9 Frankie Baker - Bob
10 Frankie Baker - Dan
11 John Brown's Dream - Bob
12 John Brown's Dream - Dan
13 John Hardy - Bob
14 John Hardy- Dan
15 John Henry - Bob
16 John Henry - Dan
17 Little Maggie - Bob
18 Little Maggie - Dan
19 Little Satchel - Bob
20 Little Satchel - Dan
21 Long Steel Rail - Bob
22 Long Steel Rail - Dan
23 Love Somebody (aka Soldier's Joy) - Bob
24 Love Somebody (aka Soldier's Joy) - Dan
25 Old Bunch of Keys - Bob
26 Old Bunch of Keys - Dan
27 Police (aka Policeman) - Bob
28 Police (aka Policeman)- Dan
29 Poor Ellen Smith - Bob
30 Poor Ellen Smith - Dan
31 Pretty Polly - Bob
32 Pretty Polly - Dan
33 Rockingham Cindy - Bob
34 Rockingham Cindy - Dan
35 Roustabout - Bob
36 Roustabout - Dan
37 Stay All Night - Bob
38 Stay All Night - Dan
39 Sweet Sunny South - Bob
40 Sweet Sunny South - Dan
41 Tempie - Bob
42 Tempie - Dan
43 Train 45 - Bob
44 Train 45 - Dan
45 Yellow Rose of Texas- Bob
46 Yellow Rose of Texas - Dan

To Access the Online Audio Go To:
www.melbay.com/30107MEB

Online Audio

1 2

Visit us on the Web at www.melbay.com — E-mail us at email@melbay.com

Acknowledgements

From Bob

Thanks to Dan, my co-author, who helped to make this idea a reality.

From Dan

All of you who have kept this music alive.

To my wife, The Lovely Miss Jennifer for continuing to support me in my chosen path.

To Bob Carlin, my co-author. He is one of my earliest inspirations and now peer and friend.

To my students who never stop teaching me as they learn.

To The Mel Bay Family and company who have continued to encourage me and provide an outlet for my works.

Play Nice!

Cover photograph of Tommy Jarrell and Fred Cockerham by Sandra Stark

Cover photograph of banjo courtesy Kevin Fore — Round Peak Banjos

All other photographers' photographs have been provided by Diane Alden from the collection of the late Ray Alden, founder of The Field Recorders' Collective (FRC).

Ray studied with Tommy and Fred and considered the FRC to be his legacy. The FRC is dedicated to the preservation and distribution of non-commercial recordings and films of traditional American folk music. http://www.fieldrecorder.com.

Table of Contents

All tunes are traditional and/or in the public domain.

Tablature has been set with makemusic - Coda Music's *finale*® software.

Introductory Notes About the Book

Welcome to *Fred Cockerham & Tommy Jarrell: Clawhammer Banjo Masters*. This is the third book in our series of transcriptions of tunes from the old masters who gave definition to our style of old time clawhammer banjo playing. The first book covered Kyle Creed (MB 22137) and the second one, the playing of Wade Ward (MB 22243). These players have passed on but not before sharing their music with the few dedicated people who traveled to meet them in the earlier days of old time music. It is through their generosity that we have this beautiful music to pass on to you and for you to pass on to the next generation of players in order to keep this tradition alive.

Please note, this book is not intended to be an instructional book. Should you find you need an instructional book, please get Dan's *Clawhammer Banjo From Scratch* (Mel Bay 20190) and the corresponding DVD's which are also available from Mel Bay. (www.melbay.com)

Also, in order to better understand the style of music being presented here, you will find Bob's *Carolina Clawhammer* DVD series a helpful reference for the playing style of the region and the players represented by it.

About Written Music - Written music has many limits when it comes to accurately representing true music. There are many subtleties and inflections that cannot be represented by the limited pallet that written music provides. Also, in one written pass through any tune, there may be countless variations of notes and techniques that would not ALL be played in one playing of the tune. This is done so you have as many options as possible to chose from when you play the tune. Learn the written music, but listen to recorded versions, too. If you listen long enough, you will find that you can sing the tune before you ever try to play it.

Creativity - Beyond The Right (*Write*) way - There is no doubt these versions will not be the only version you come upon as you journey through the old time music world; nor will these be the ones you always want to play or hear. These tabs are intended to be a starting point, not the ending. In reality, there is no one right way to play any tune. Everything is open to your interpretation. If there is a right way it is the way you like it. HOWEVER, if you are interested in an historic interpretation of these tunes and their development since being brought into the common repertoire from a respected source, these transcriptions will get you well on your way.

About the Audio Files

Listening to the tunes is at least as important as playing them from a written source. You will find audio files for each tune on line at to www.melbay.com/30107MEB in order to give you a recorded example of the banjo tabs as they are written here. Each of us plays each tune one time through. The recorded version of the tune is intended to be close to but not necessarily exactly as written. In most cases, the recorded tempos are slower than performance speed and intended to be for demonstration purposes only.

About the Tunes

The tunes in this volume represents some of the most common tunes played by Fred Cockerham and Tommy Jarrell. There are two tabs for each tune.

The first tab has been transcribed from Fred or Tommy's playing by Bob Carlin and accurately represents their own playing. In many instances you will find some alternate measures suggested along with the complete tab. These will help you create variations and are reflective of the variety and richness that was associated with their music.

The second tab was written by Dan and reflects more modern methods of getting Fred or Tommy's sounds. You will find some things easier here – there are fewer *drags* or *alternate string pull-off's* for instance – but other things more difficult in order to recreate the sounds you expect to hear in Fred and Tommy's playing without some of the techniques they used regularly. In all cases, these tunes should be playable by most players having good basic clawhammer banjo skills though you may have to add a technique or two to your *toolbox.*

Reading the Tablature

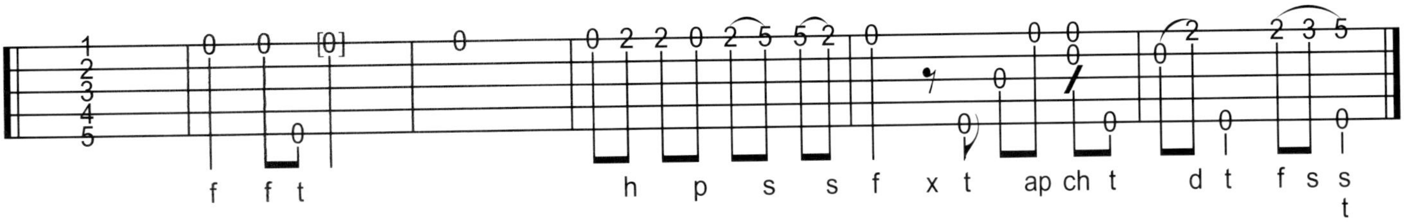

This book is written with a type of music notation known as tablature. Reading tablature is in many ways easier for fretted instruments than reading standard music notation.

The lines of the staff indicate the strings of the banjo. The numbers tell you the fret numbers on that string. The top line of the staff represents the 1st string of your banjo and the bottom line the 5th (short) string.

The second measure shows the notes used. A quarter note counts as 1 beat. Eighth notes count as 1/2 beat each so 2 eighth notes = one quarter, and a half note counts for 2 beats or 2 times a quarter note. The next measure shows a whole note which counts as 4 beats.

The letters under the notes indicate whether you use the finger - "f" or the thumb - "t" of your right hand to play the note. An "x" (5th measure) indicates silence used both for rests and skipped beats — i.e. you don't play this note but your hand keeps moving down and up even so.

The h, p and s give playing directions for your left hand. The "h" is for a *hammer-on*, "p" is for a *pull-off* and the "s" indicates a *slide*. I also use a "slur" (the curve above the notes) for the slide.

The "ap" under the note in measure 5 indicates an *alternate string pull off* where you pluck the string noted with your left hand even though you didn't play it with the right. The "ch" under the next note indicates a *chuck* or *cluck*. The *chuck* sound has become very popular these days and sounds like a clicking, *chking* sound hence its name. It adds a rhythmic texture to your playing and if used judiciously (i.e. not used too often) can make your playing more interesting. In tab I have chosen to indicate it by a slash " / " within a chord. You play it by first striking the chord with your normal playing finger then immediately deadening the notes by resting the next finger of your playing hand against that same string. In the next measure, the "d" indicates a *drag* where you are playing two or more consecutive strings with the same finger over one beat by slowing down your stroke to take a full beat to play all of the notes with your fingernail. This leads us to what is referred to as the *Galax Lick.*

Galax Lick - Here you are actually taking 2 beats to complete the down-up hand motion of clawhammer stroke instead of the usual one beat. Your finger plays the first notes of the series on the downstroke — either an *h, p, s,* on the first string or a *drag* (*d*) of the finger across multiple strings — followed by a continued motion when the thumb plays the fifth string as your hand comes up (see the last measure of the tab example) putting the fifth string at the beginning of a beat instead of the end.

Notes with no marking under them usually fit the rule that if the note is on the first half of the beat, it is played with your finger, the second half of the beat, it is played with your thumb.

Bob's Method

In my part of this book, you'll find my transcriptions of a large part of Fred or Tommy's banjo tunes played the way they played them. I am proud that this is the first guide to capture such intimate details of their banjo style on some of the core tunes from their region.

To Northern banjoists of the late 1950's and early 1960's, after "Uncle" Wade Ward, Tommy Jarrell, Fred Cockerham, Kyle Creed and their *Round Peak* ilk became the old time music gurus.

Ever since my first trip to the South in 1975, I realized the importance of learning how the traditional musicians played. One didn't have to always imitate or even keep within the confines of a *traditional* style, but, it seemed to sure help your music if you understood how the tradition worked. As long as you "knew how a banjo was played," you'd be alright. That first journey opened up a whole world of music to me, leading to my attendance of summer fiddlers' conventions and multiple visits to the homes of those musicians I admired, both young and old.

One of the obvious rules of learning directly from the older players was that it then became my job to pass that information along to someone else. It's a role that I've taken seriously. I was handed a precious object—a tune, a technique—and then asked to treat that musical object with respect. Fred Cockerham once said to "tell 'em [after he was gone] that Fred Cockerham used to could play a banjo, but, he can't anymore." It has become my duty, along with a handful of others making the same journey, to care-take the tradition for future generations and to share what makes it tick.

This book is another piece in my passing along the tradition to a new generation of players. I hope you find the information contained in this guide useful in your quest of clawhammer enlightenment. I find the more I know the more enjoyable music making becomes.

Have fun with this information and may it lead you another step in your learning process.

----Bob Carlin, Lexington, NC

A note about tunings — (adapted from the comments of Charles Faurot who was one of the first to head south to record the masters while they were still alive.)

"When I started playing the banjo in the mid-'50's and when I started serious recording in 1965, there weren't enormous lists of banjo tunings around. No one seemed to feel that the G tuning was different from the A tuning. I still feel that it is the relation between the strings and not their actual pitch that is important.

If you are trying to learn these tunes from their original recordings, please be aware that, during those sessions, these folks never used a capo. Furthermore, they never seemed to be pitched to standard A=440. You tune one string to the key they were playing in, e.g. third string up to match the recording and tune the other strings to that."

(A = 440 is an arbitrary pitch for A established as the standard late in the 1800's. Prior to that A was closer to 436 and varied by orchestra. Some orchestras in Europe have recently pushed A to 444 as the standard pitch, including piano. dl)

Dan's Method

Though I was raised with music in my home, I first began to play clawhammer banjo seriously around 1985. I had both the guidance of books as well a wealth of recordings of current players as well as masters since passed on. County Records had released its *Clawhammer Banjo 1, 2 and 3* lp's (now available as CD's and downloads) to hear the sound of the older players. Recordings by bands such as *The Highwoods Stringband* and *The Horseflies* and performers such as co-author *Bob Carlin* and others made hearing the *modern* versions of clawhammer readily available as well.

In the 1980's I was dancing with the *Coal Country Cloggers* and traveling to more festivals. Shortly after that I found myself working for a store that sold these great old time records and I went to some of the best gatherings of the day as a vendor and student of the style. This gave me incredible opportunities to both meet and play with some of the most influential players of the day at a time when I could best benefit from their influence and input. It was an opportunity to *go to the mountain* so to speak and become immersed in and embraced by old time music on its home turf. Even so, I was a link away from people such as Fred Cockerham, Tommy Jarrell and their contemporaries. While most folks said I did fine, I still never got quite the experience or examples of those who went directly to visit those old timers in person.

So, I came up with versions of many popular jam tunes by simple trial and error, using the available recordings and a good many jam tapes to guide my sound and the instruction of my local mentors — including Kevin Enoch, Mark Olitsky and Pete Smakula, then my boss — to guide my technique. Little did I know then how much I had changed and perhaps even missed.

The development of this book has shown me how much more I can still get out of these tunes and how much growth still exists for me within the confines of what we have come to call *Old Time Music*. Through seeing and working with Bob's accurate transcriptions of Fred or Tommy's tunes and hearing their technique more in depth as I listen closer to their own recordings, I have gained new insight into my playing that I would have never been aware of had it not been for the tabs presented here. You will notice that my versions don't tend to have as many of the dragged notes or galax lick nor do I use the SO often used alternate string pull-off's where you pluck an un-played string with your left hand — techniques you will find often in Bob's transcriptions of both Fred and Tommy's playing. They are great techniques and I'm still learning! Hopefully you all are too.

So, in my *ignorance* of what Fred, Tommy and so many of their contemporaries did, I found different ways to skin the same ... ah, banjo! Even Bob Carlin commented that he was surprised at how *Round Peak-ey* my versions sounded when he played out my transcriptions. In my more modern styled tabs of their playing you will find some more ideas to include in your variations which shows how music—even *Old Time Music* is a fluid and living tradition which respects where it has come from while recognizing growth and development. It was Kyle Creed who said, "you folks can do that if you like, but it just puts more work into it that way. ...But, you can do that if you want." It applies here as well.

Don't worry if you don't play these tabs note for note as written. This music is to be enjoyed and interpreted through your hands too. It is great to have the masters' guidance but in the end, you need to be true to yourself and enjoy the music. Just remember ...

Play nice!
Dan Levenson, Vinton, OH

TOMMY JARRELL AND FRED COCKERHAM

Volume Three of our Clawhammer Masters series fittingly presents the banjo playing of two musicians joined at the hip in the old time music consciousness, Tommy Jarrell and Fred Cockerham. Although both were fine fiddle players, we focus within these pages on their playing of the down-stroking banjo style popular in their region.

Thomas Jefferson Jarrell was born in 1901, the son of Ben and Susan Jarrell. His father was the fiddler for *Da Costa Woltz and his Southern Broadcasters*, a string band that recorded nine 78rpm records for Gennett in 1927. Oddly enough, Ben did not push Tommy to play. It remained for Baugie Cockerham, ten years Tommy's senior, to start him off on the banjo at age eight.

Tommy told Ray Alden about Baugie: "He stayed out at our house one year. Granddaddy hired him by the month to help us farm, and he's the fellow learnt me the first tune ever I played on anything, old timey *Ruben*. He tuned the banjo down so there wouldn't be but one string to note."

Soon after, Tommy's father brought him a small banjo whose neck was stained with pokeberry juice.

Fred Cockerham, one of the seven children of Elias and Betty Jane Cockerham, was born on November 3, 1905. He was the only member of his generation from the *Round Peak* community to attempt the difficult life of a professional rural musician.

Fred's family was interested in and encouraged music, as Fred recalled: "My Daddy, he weighed about 150 I guess, and wore a size six shoe, and he could dance, just like lightning. He would take two straws out of a broom and sit down right in front of me. I'd be on the fiddle or banjo, he'd play every note I'd play with those straws on the strings between where I'd pick and note. He had music in him."

As with Tommy, there were local pickers who helped to develop and fine-tune Fred's musical talents. Mal Smith, a banjo player who lived close by, played with Fred for several years after returning from World War I. Mal taught Fred a banjo tune that later became his solo showpiece, *Roustabout*.

However, there was one person whose playing so impressed Fred that he felt: "If I couldn't learn to mock [him], why I'd just as soon quit." Charlie Lowe's handling of the banjo was so inspiring that Fred worked hard to change his "framming" style to be more like the technique used by Charlie.

Charlie was regarded as the standard by which all other area banjo players were measured. He brought drop thumb clawhammer to a new level of excellence using a double note technique that incorporated an uncanny sense of timing, speed and deadly accuracy. Charlie was born in 1878 in the Round Peak area, two years Ben Jarrell's senior. He was warmly regarded and, at the same time, noted for his idiosyncrasies.

Tommy remembered Charlie: "You go to Charlie Lowe's house when it come eating time and you had to eat. Oh, he's a kind-hearted kind of a feller. He's like me; never did have much of anything, but he's willing to divide whatever he had with anybody. Wasn't no better feller than Charlie Lowe. But now when he got through playing, now he was through! Wasn't no use [sic] asking him to play another." Fred Cockerham added: "No sir. He'd put that music under his arm and say to his children, 'Come on boys, girls, let's go,' and God, they's ready too."

For years, Charlie had played with Ben Jarrell, but by the time Tommy was 15, he became good enough to be the fiddler with whom Charlie worked the local dances. Fred Cockerham, four years younger than Tommy, began to be influenced by Charlie's banjo playing at this time.

By 1916, Fred's musical talent was beginning to be recognized, as he recalled: "Tommy and Uncle Charlie Lowe used'a play up at Uncle Charlie Jarrell's. I guess I was about 15 then. I'd be there for a dance they were playing for. Uncle Charlie Lowe, he's just as steady as a clock, every once in awhile he'd say, 'I-gad Fred, rest me one.' He was an awful good fella."

Fred Cockerham had married Eva Gaylean when they were still teenagers. After living for many years in and around Galax, Virginia, in 1959, Fred and Eva moved to Lowgap, North Carolina, close to the Round Peak community. This was the beginning of a period of bad luck for Fred. In 1960 a doctor operated on both of his cataracts simultaneously, instead of the normal technique of one at a time, leaving Cockerham only able to see vague forms.

But, people from the community rallied around. Charlie Lowe came over to encourage Fred Cockerham and Kyle Creed built him the Formica® covered fretless banjo that now resides in the Smithsonian Institution along with Tommy's fiddle. Soon after, Kyle reformed the band of their youth and named it the *Camp Creek Boys*, after the stream that flowed near their old home place. This old time band, including Fred, Kyle, Earnest East, Paul Sutphin and Verlin Clifton, was so powerful that they often won against the more popular bluegrass bands at a time when there was no separate divisions at fiddlers' contests.

Tommy Jarrell retired in 1966 after 41 years with the state, only to have his wife Nina pass away the year after. About that time, Tommy's son B.F. (Benjamin Franklin, born 1933), working as a radio D.J. near Durham, read that graduate student Alan Jabbour was interested in old time fiddlers. B.F., meeting Alan at a fiddlers contest told him: "You ought to hear my daddy play the fiddle." Alan, who became director of the Library of Congress' American Folklife Division, visited and recorded Tommy.

It wasn't until the mid 1960's that record producers Richard Nevins and Charlie Faurot, in an attempt to recreate *Da Costa Woltz's Southern Broadcasters,* put Fred (taking Da Costa Woltz's part) together with Tommy (taking his father Ben's part) and Oscar Jenkins (taking his father Frank's part) for three albums on County.

Soon, many young musicians began making pilgrimages to see Tommy Jarrell, which kept him enjoying the music until his death at the end of January 1985. He won many awards, including the NEA's National Heritage Fellowship Award.

Although fewer young people visited Fred than Tommy in order time to learn their style of music, Cockerham was tremendously giving to those who did come. Most tried to give something back, as did Barry and Sharon Poss in 1973 when they arranged with a doctor for an operation that restored much of Fred's lost vision.

Fred died four months short of his 75th birthday, on July 8, 1980.

(Excerpted from notes by Ray Alden, http://www.fieldrecorder.com/docs/notes/cockerham_alden.htm and http://www.fieldrecorder.com/docs/notes/jarrell_alden.htm.)

DISCOGRAPHY/SOURCES

Come and Go With Me, Tommy Jarrell, County Records

Tommy and Fred, Fred Cockerham, County Records

High Atmosphere, Fred Cockerham, Rounder Records

More Clawhammer Banjo, Tommy Jarrell, Fred Cockerham, County Records

The North Carolina Banjo Collection, Tommy Jarrell, Rounder Records

Fred Cockerham, Field Recorders Collective

Clawhammer Banjo, Fred Cockerham, County Records

Stay All Night, Fred Cockerham, County Records

Clawhammer Banjo Volume Three, County Records

As Time Draws Near

as played by Tommy Jarrell on *Come and Go With Me*

G Tuning
gDGBD

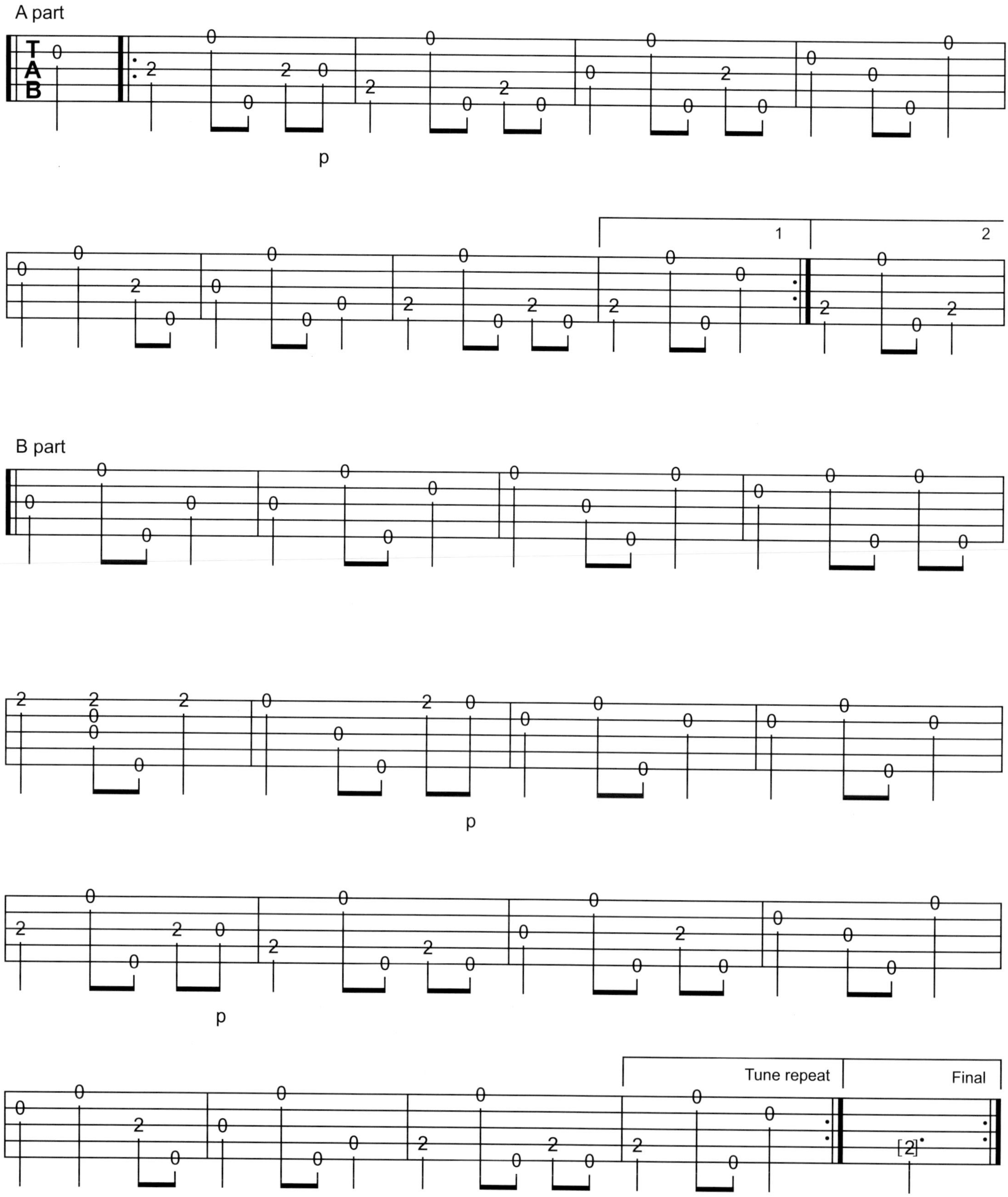

As Time Draws Near

as played by Dan

G Tuning
gDGBD

A part

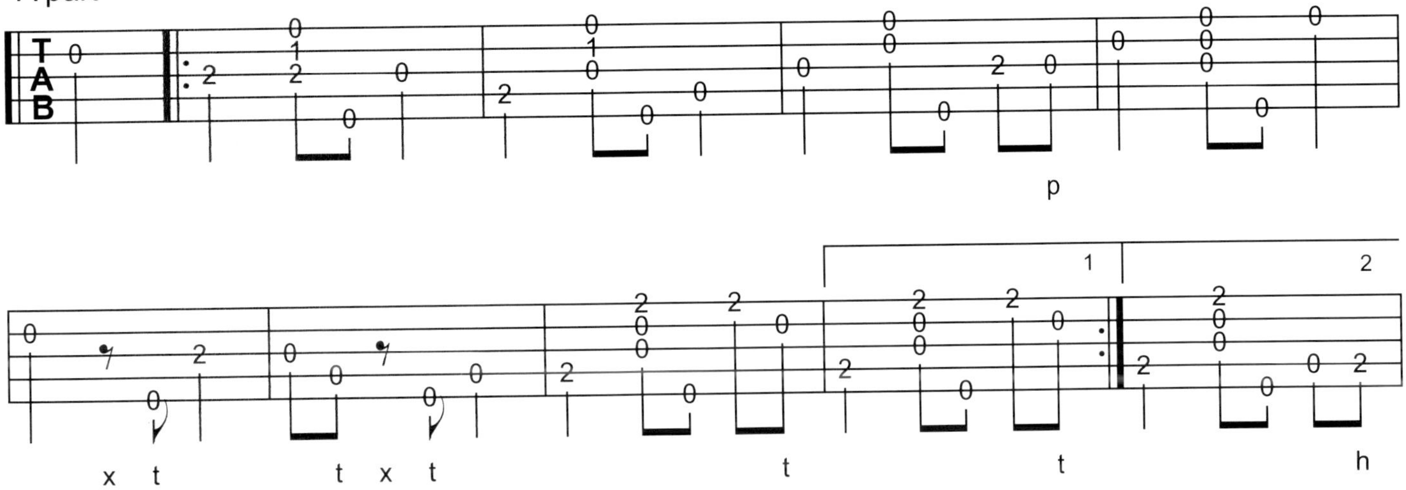

B part

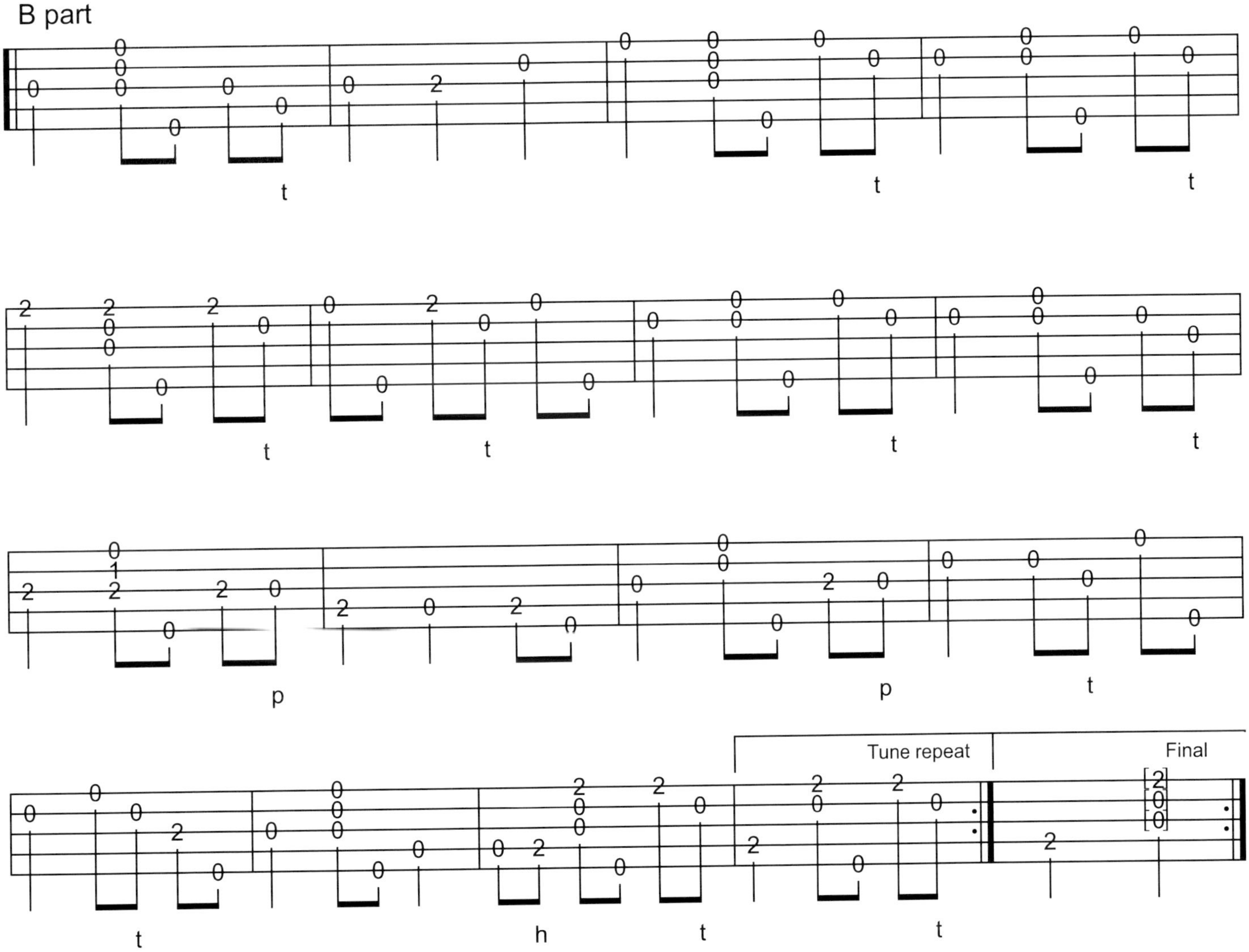

Back Step Cindy

as played by Tommy Jarrell on *Come and Go With Me*

Double D tuning
aDADE (double C capo 2)

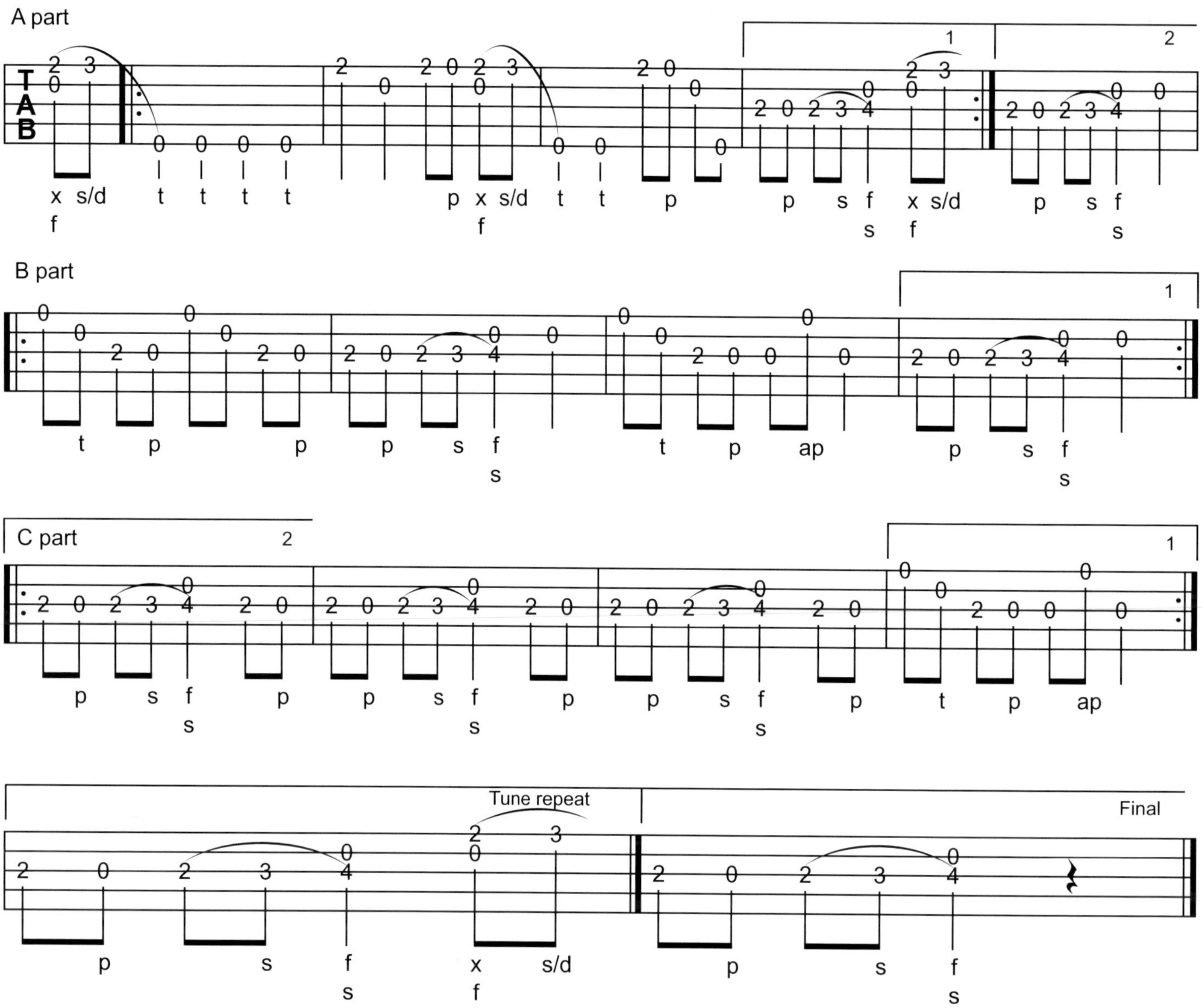

One commonly used technique by Tommy Jarrell, Fred Cockerham and the other players from the Round Peak area is, on the first string, to slide up to notes before they are struck as part of a "drag" across strings two and one. The pick-up into the first measure of Back Step Cindy is a good example of this technique.

Back Step Cindy

as played by Dan

Double D tuning
aDADE (double C capo 2)

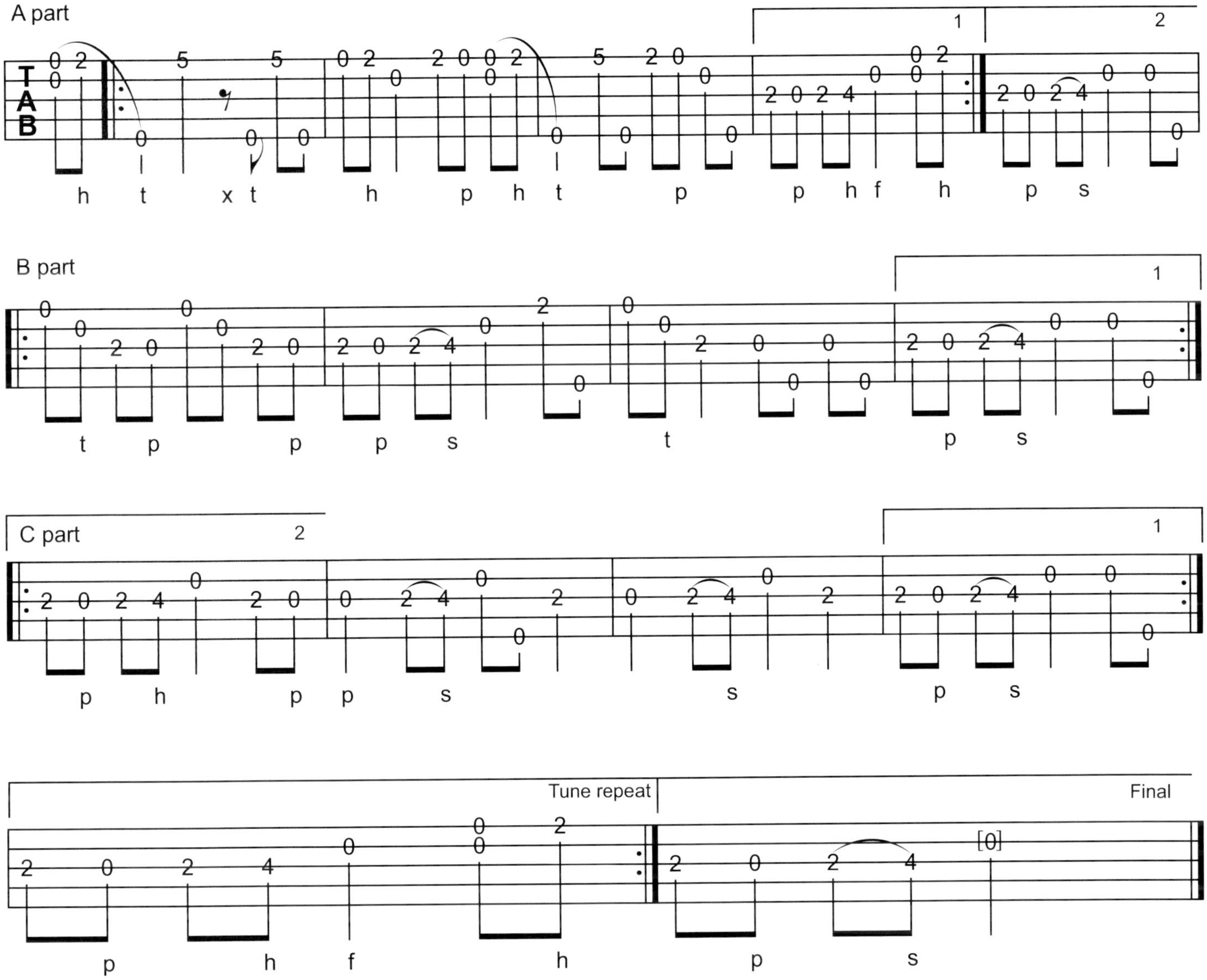

Big Eyed Rabbit

as played by Fred Cockerham on *Tommy and Fred*

A tuning
aEAC#E (G capo 2)

A part

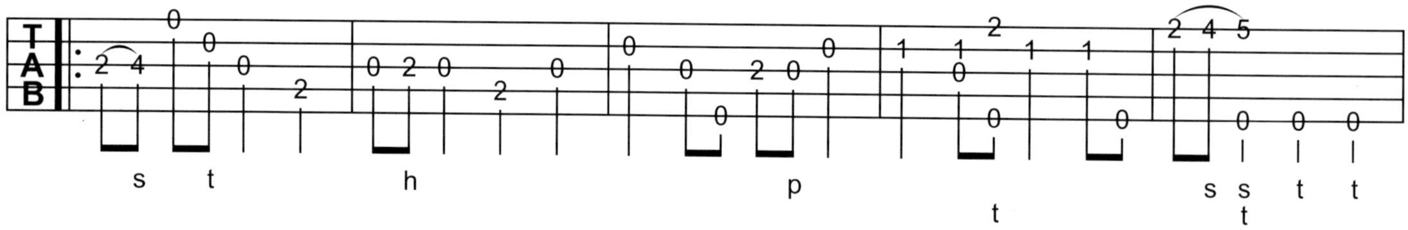

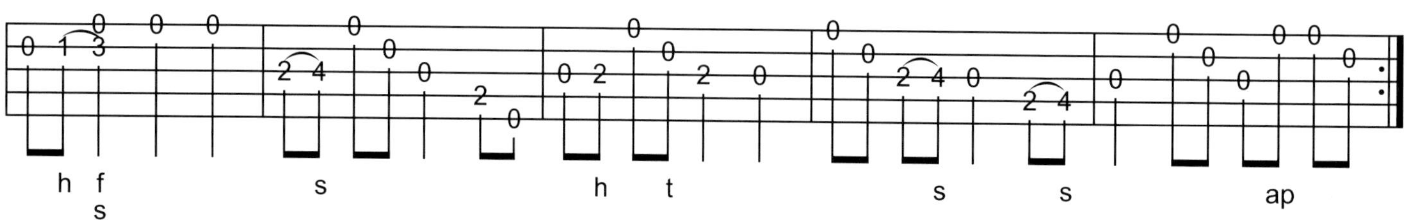

B part

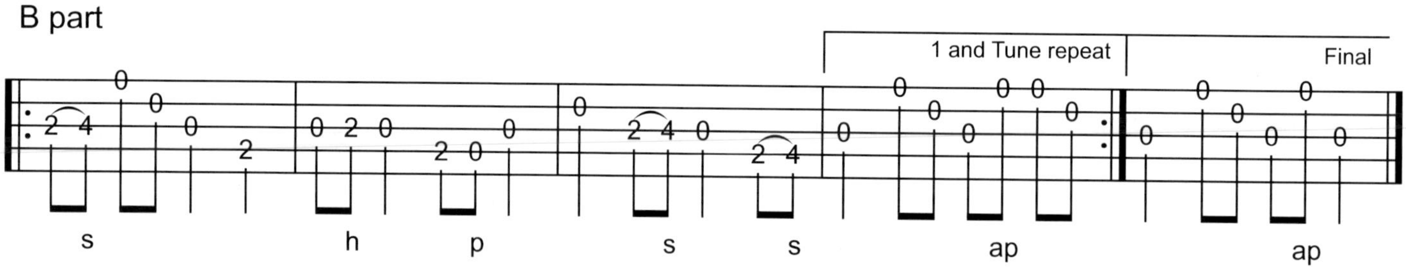

Alternate A part - first 2 measures

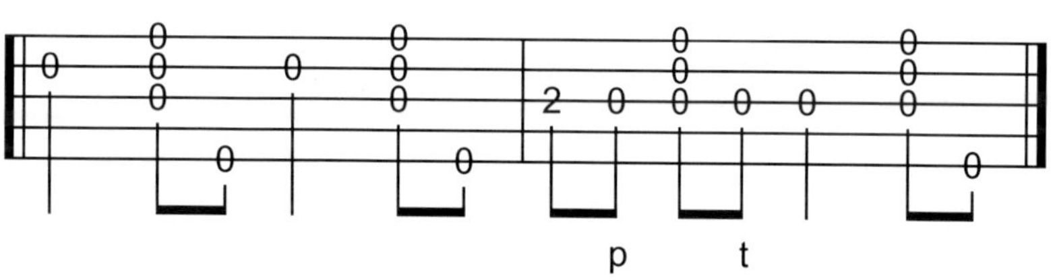

Big Eyed Rabbit

as played by Dan

A tuning
aEAC#E (G capo 2)

A part

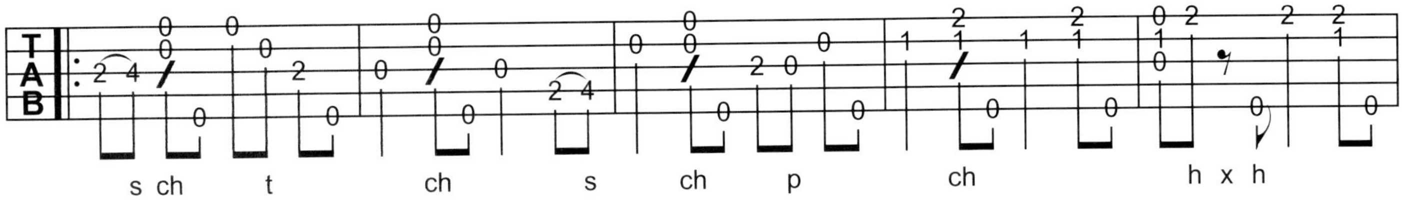

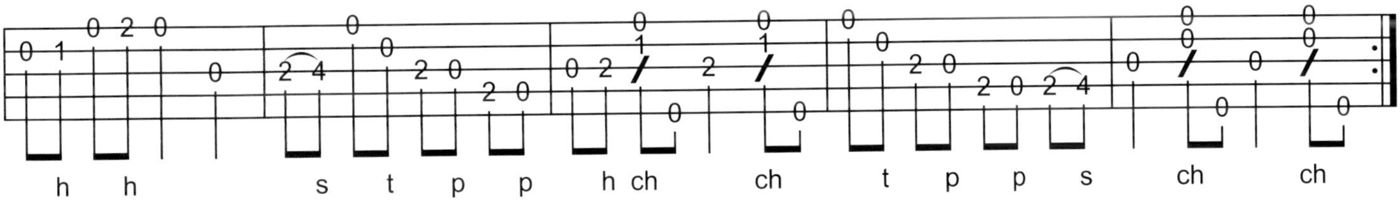

B part

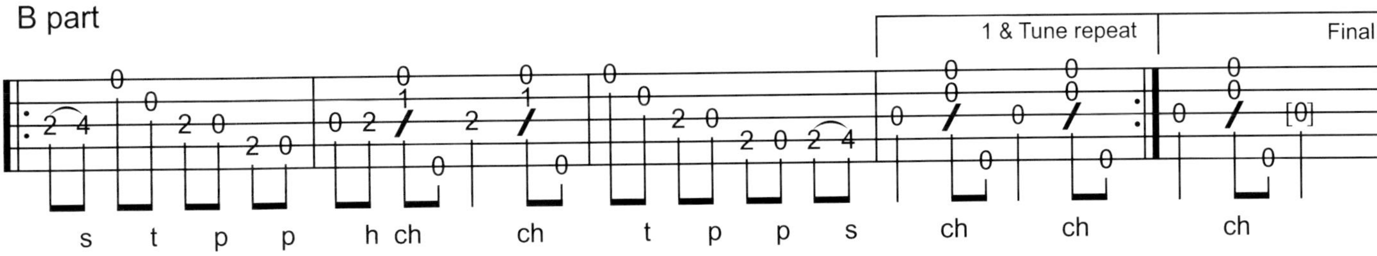

The slash "/" and "*ch*" notation that you see in the chords including that slash indicate a *chuck* or *cluck* sound which is actually a deadening of a string right as you play it. You are sounding and stopping that string almost at once.

Some folks consider this too "modern" of a technique or at least an overuse of a happy accident. You can choose to use it or not but if you do, generally less is more. Use it as an accent, not a regular over and over thing.

Ducks on the Millpond

as played by Tommy Jarrell on *Come and Go With Me*

Double D tuning
aDADE (double C capo 2)

A part

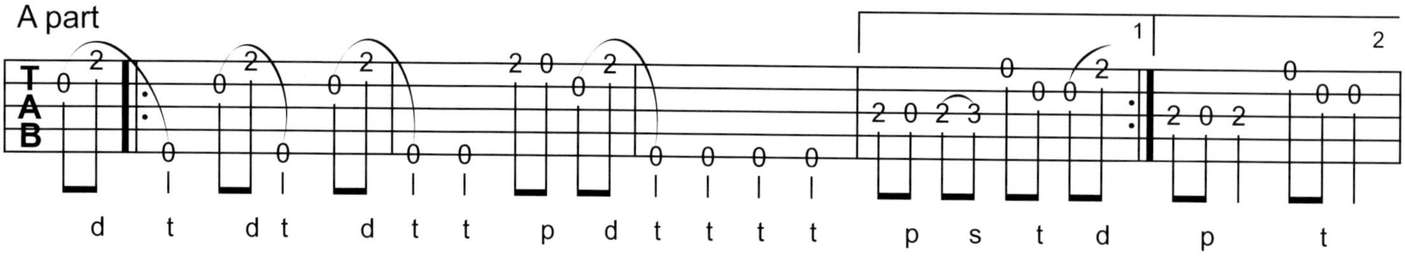

B part

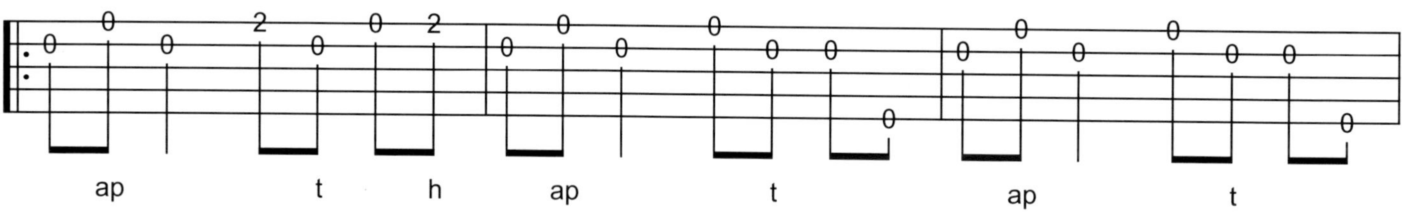

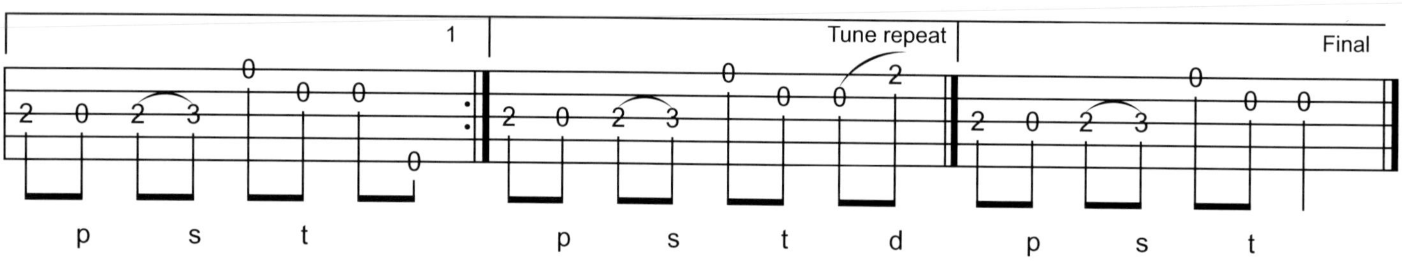

Ducks on the Millpond

as played by Dan

Double D tuning
aDADE (double C capo 2)

A part

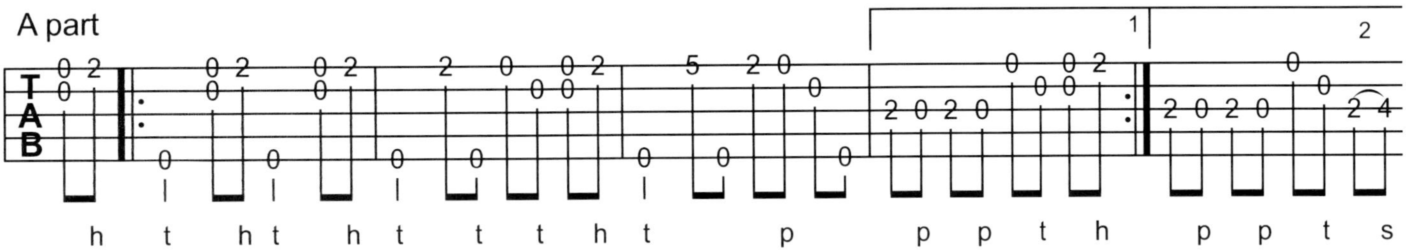

B part

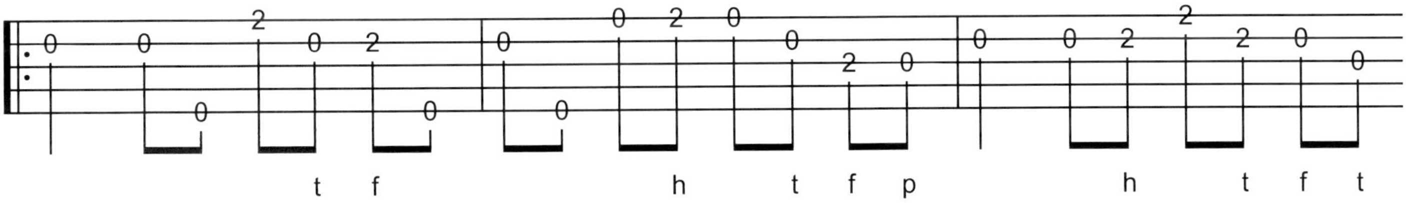

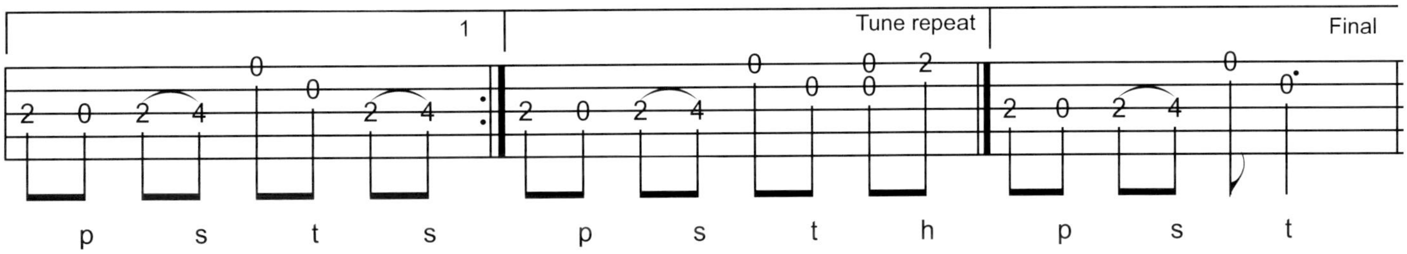

Frankie Baker

as played by Fred Cockerham on *High Atmosphere*

g#C#F#BE
f#BEAD - capo 2

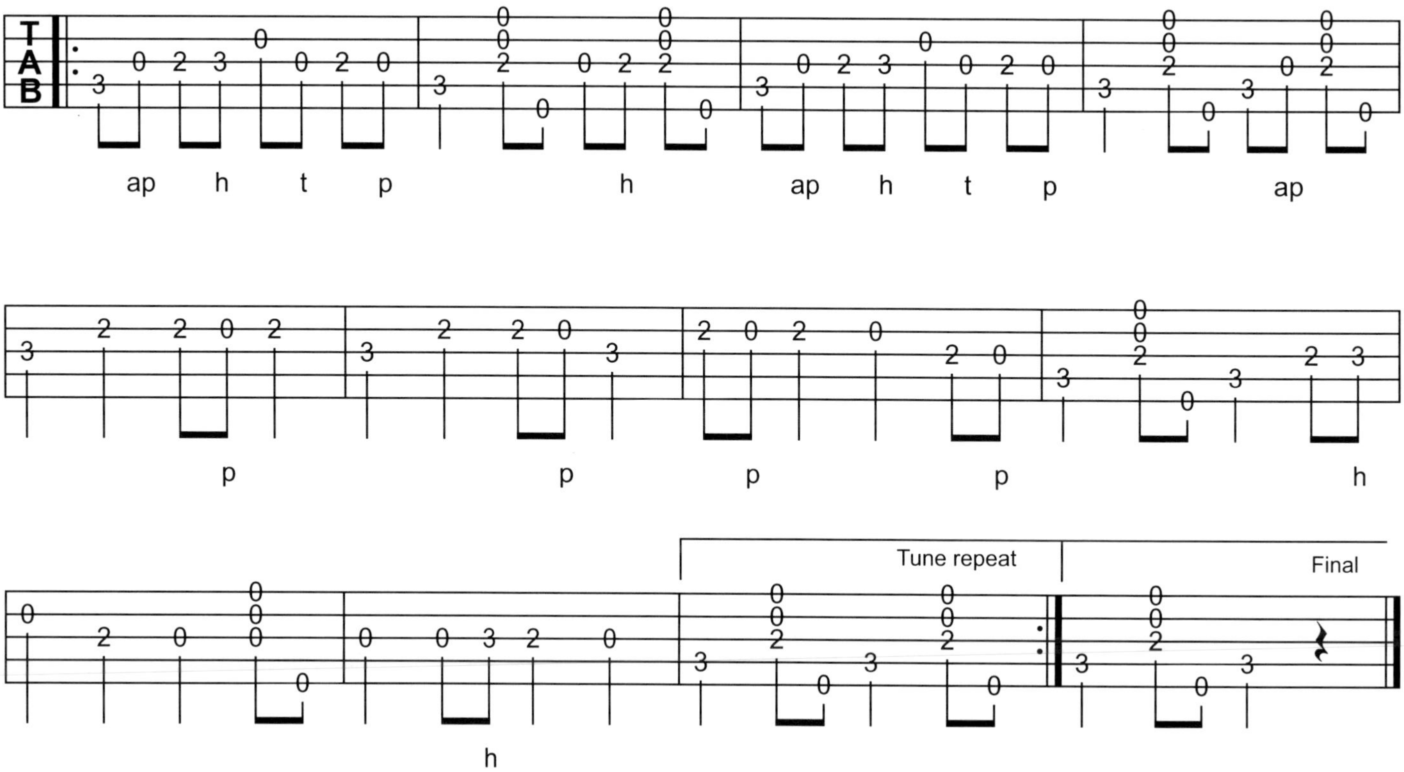

Fred and Eva Cockerham, Low Gap, NC
Photographer and date unknown

Frankie Baker

as played by Dan

g#C#F#BE
f#BEAD - capo 2

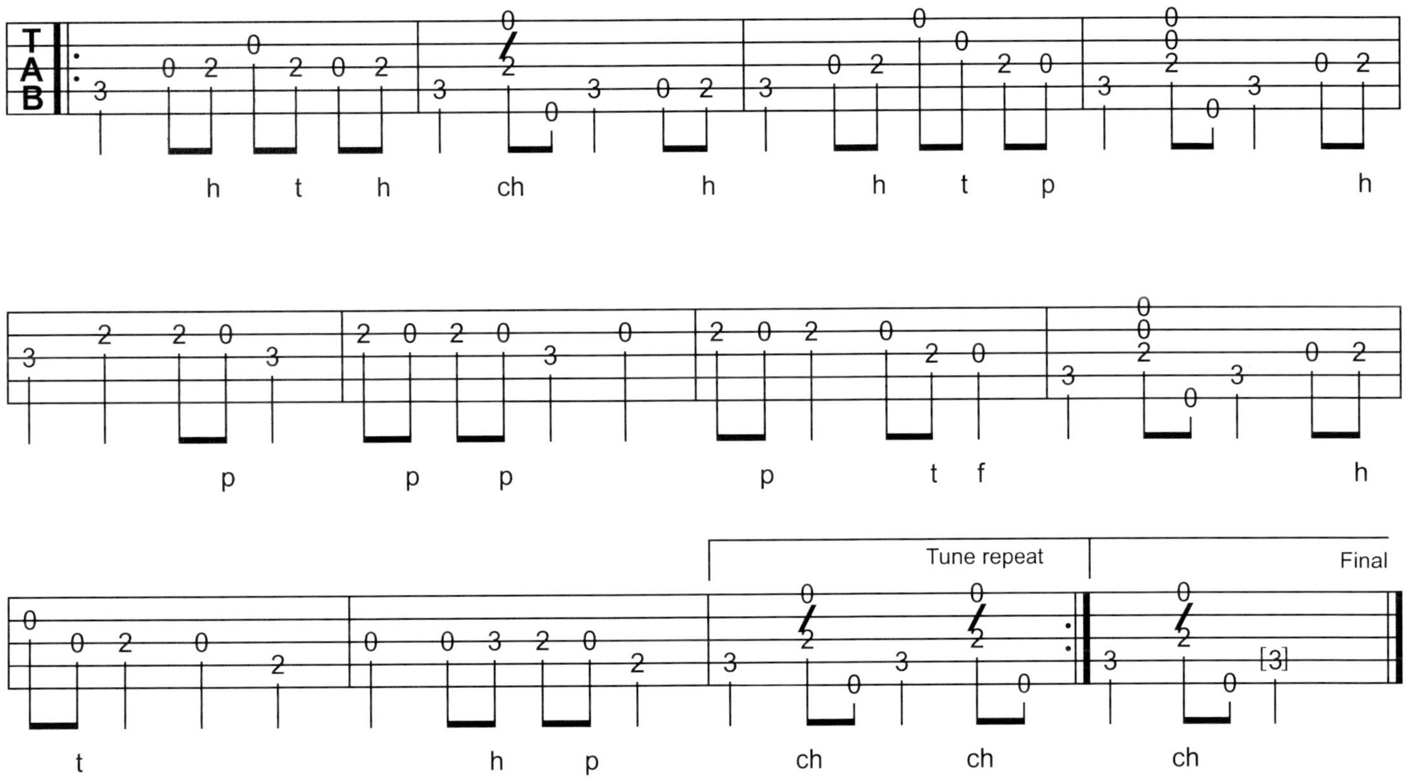

Again, use the *chuck* (*ch* - /) sparingly. I listed it in some chords but not all. Pick and choose as to the ones you feel it in.

John Brown's Dream

as played by Tommy Jarrell on *More Clawhammer Banjo*

Key of A tuning - aAAC#E
(gGGBD capo 2)

A part

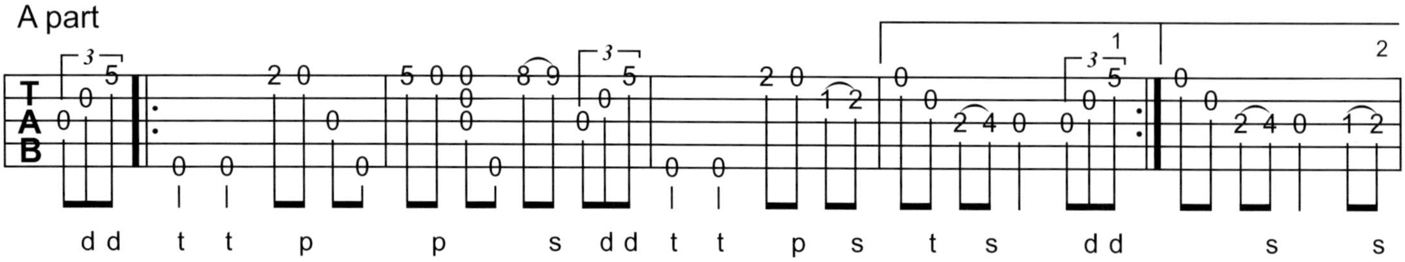

B part

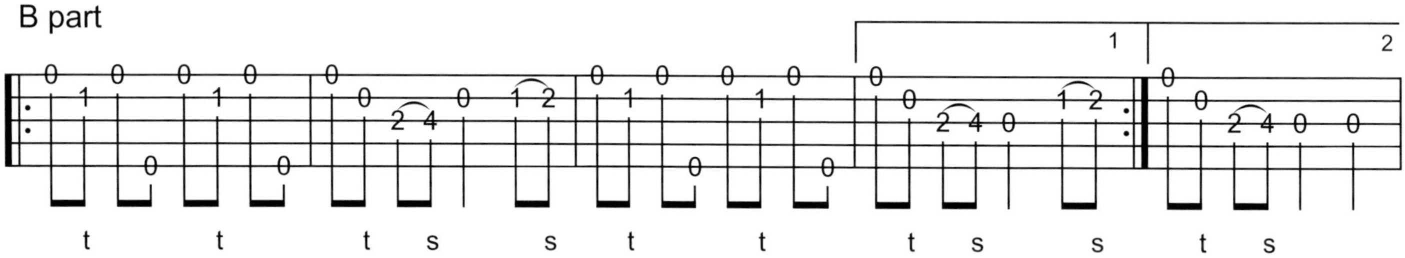

C part

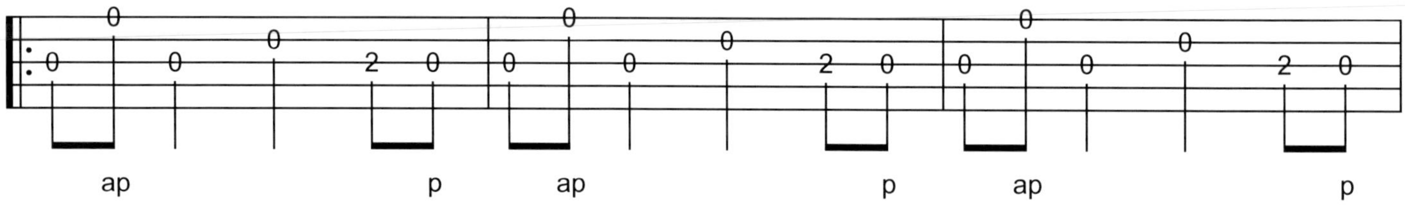

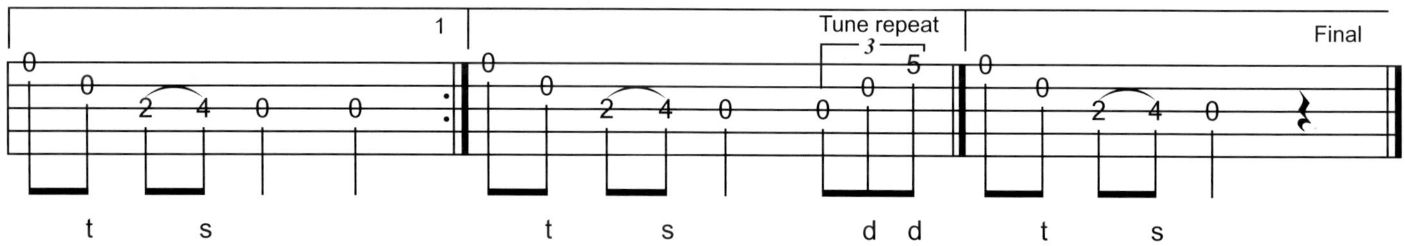

John Brown's Dream

as played by Dan

Key of A tuning - aAAC#E
(gGGBD capo 2)

A part

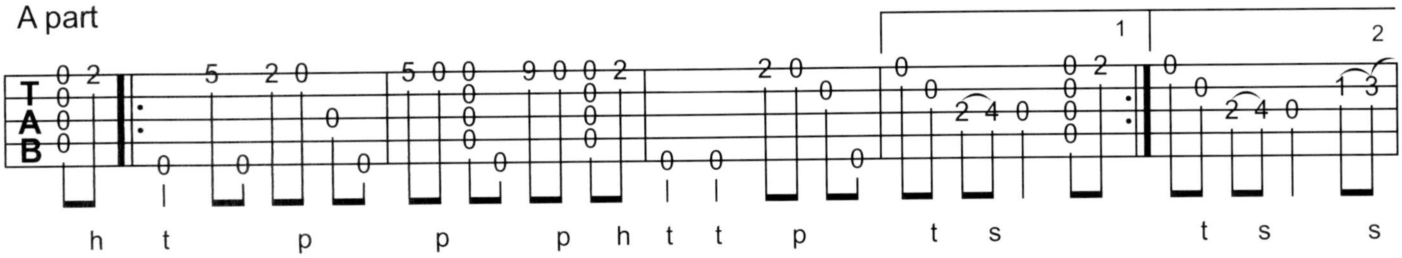

B part

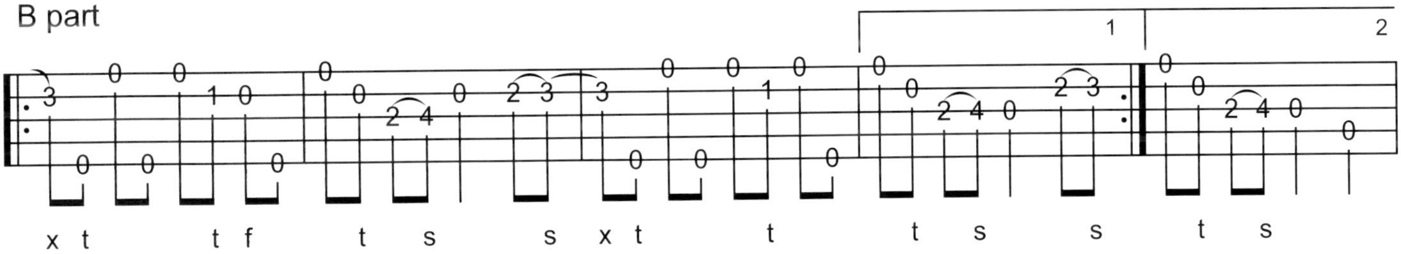

C part

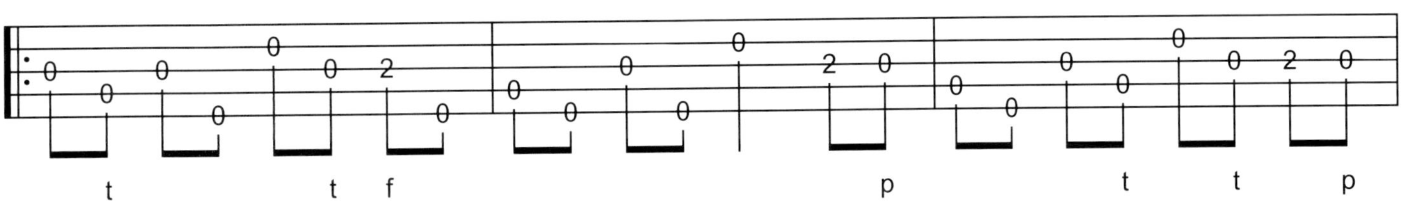

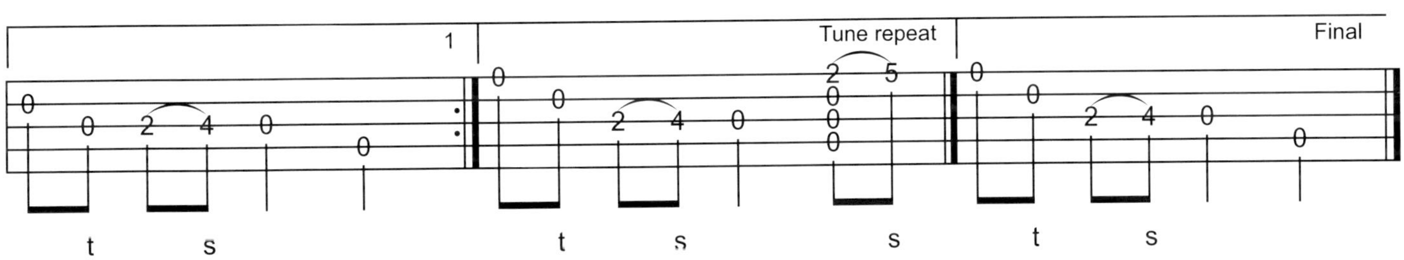

In Tommy's recording you can hear the low A (4th) string sounding as an undertone throughout a lot of this piece. Bob doesn't actually strike it in his transcription of Tommy's playing but I felt that I wanted to actively use this note to accentuate the ringing of that pitch.

John Hardy

as played by Tommy Jarrell on *Come and Go With Me*

A tuning
aEAC#E (G capo 2)

A part

B part

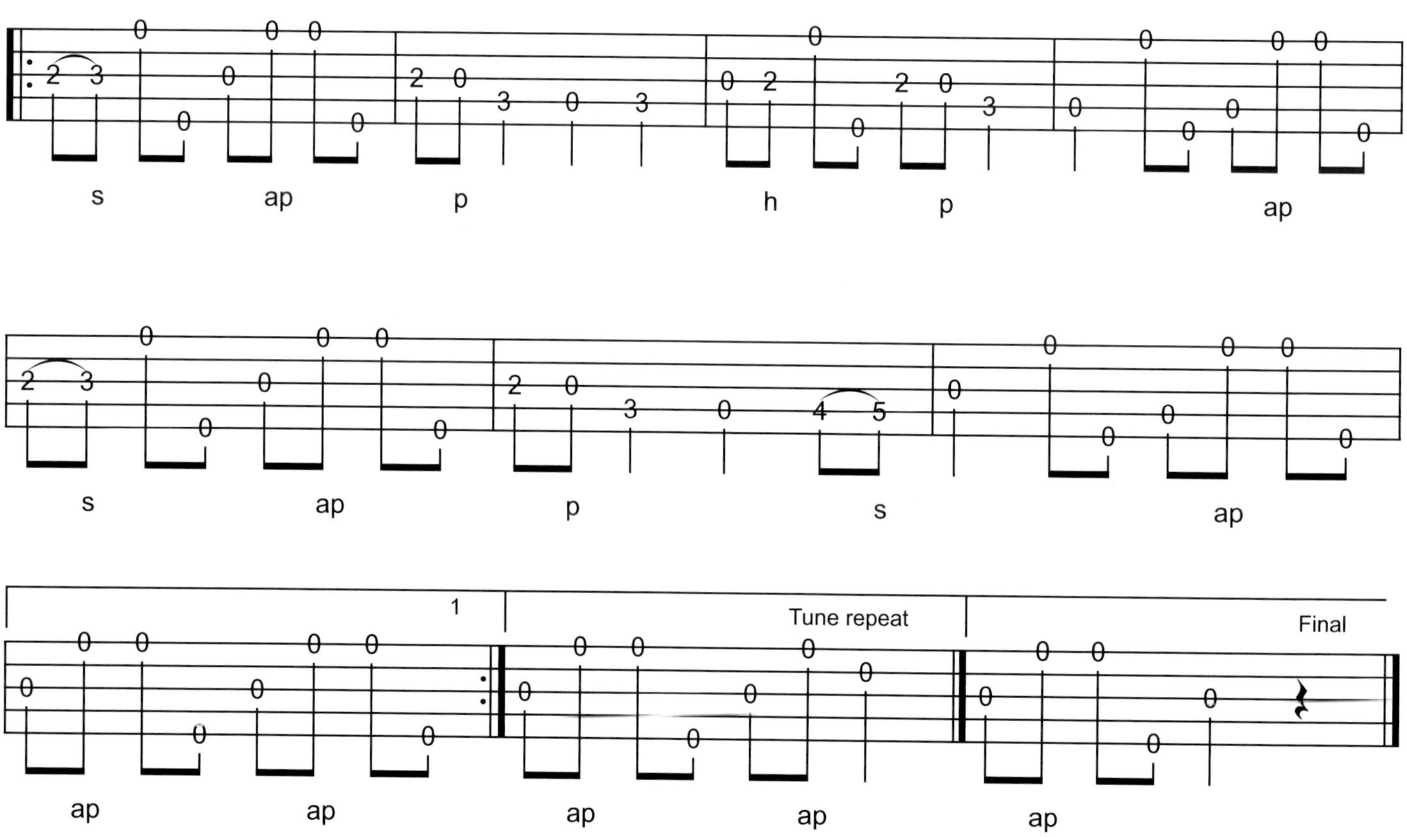

John Hardy

as played by Dan

A tuning
aEAC#E (G capo 2)

A part

B part

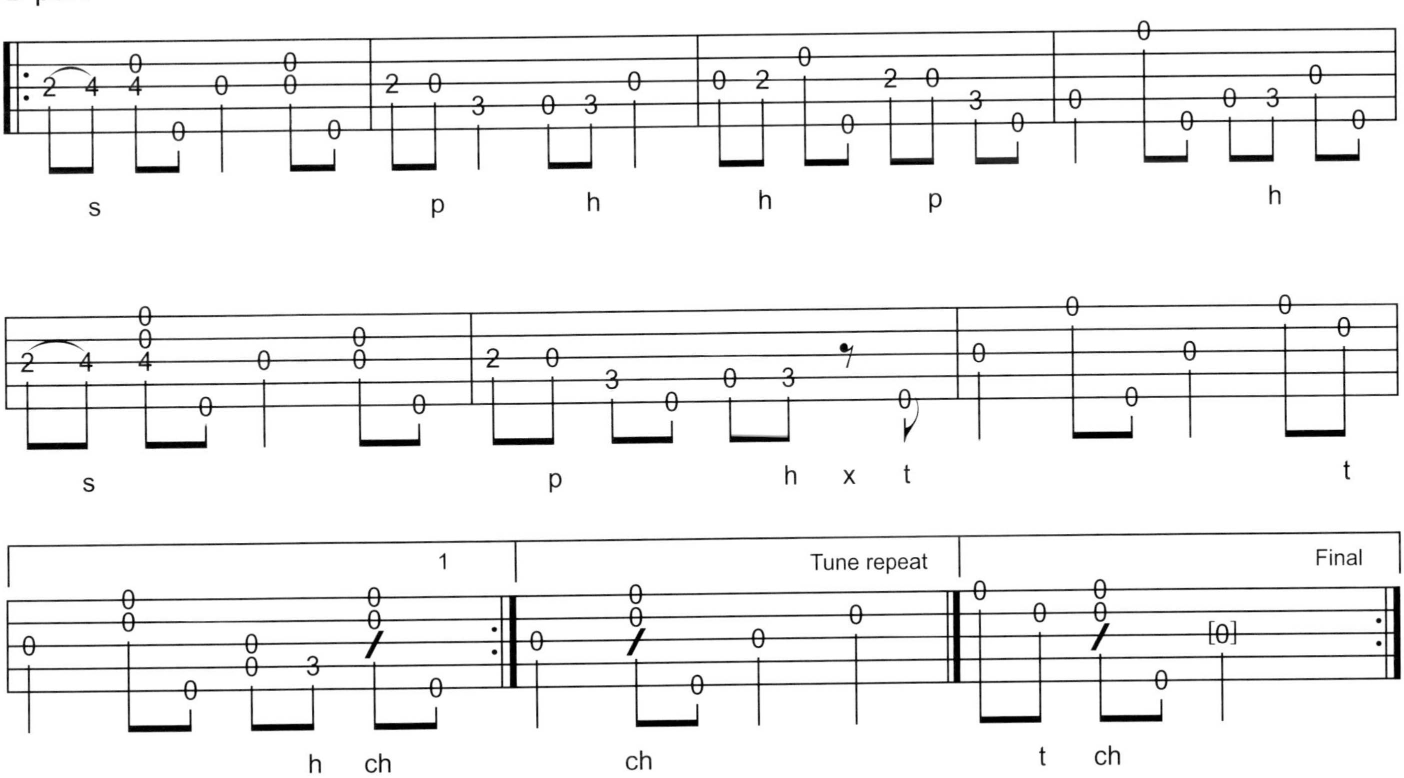

John Henry

as played by Tommy Jarrell - Private tape - 1980
North Carolina Banjo Collection

A tuning
aEAC#E (G capo 2)

A part

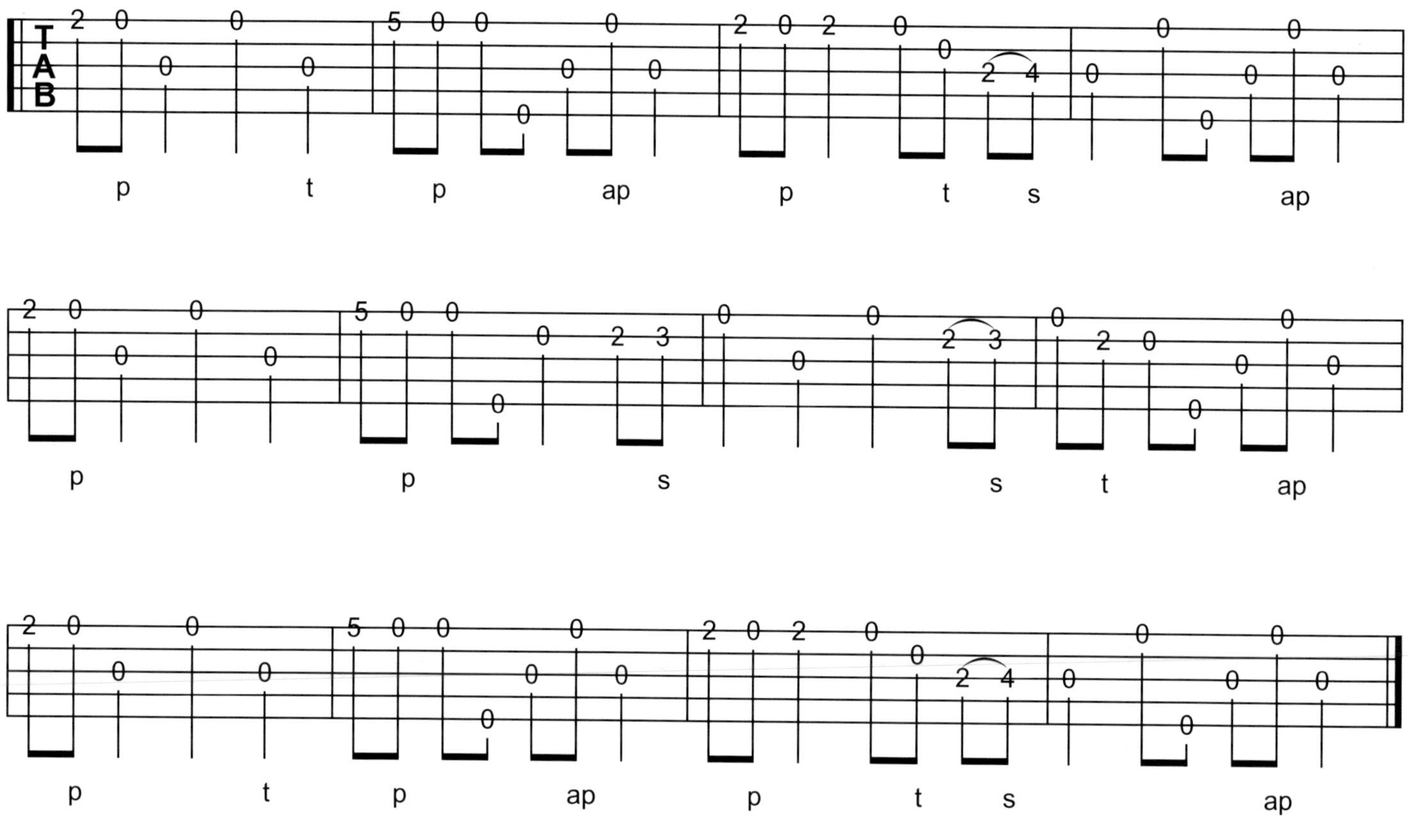

B part

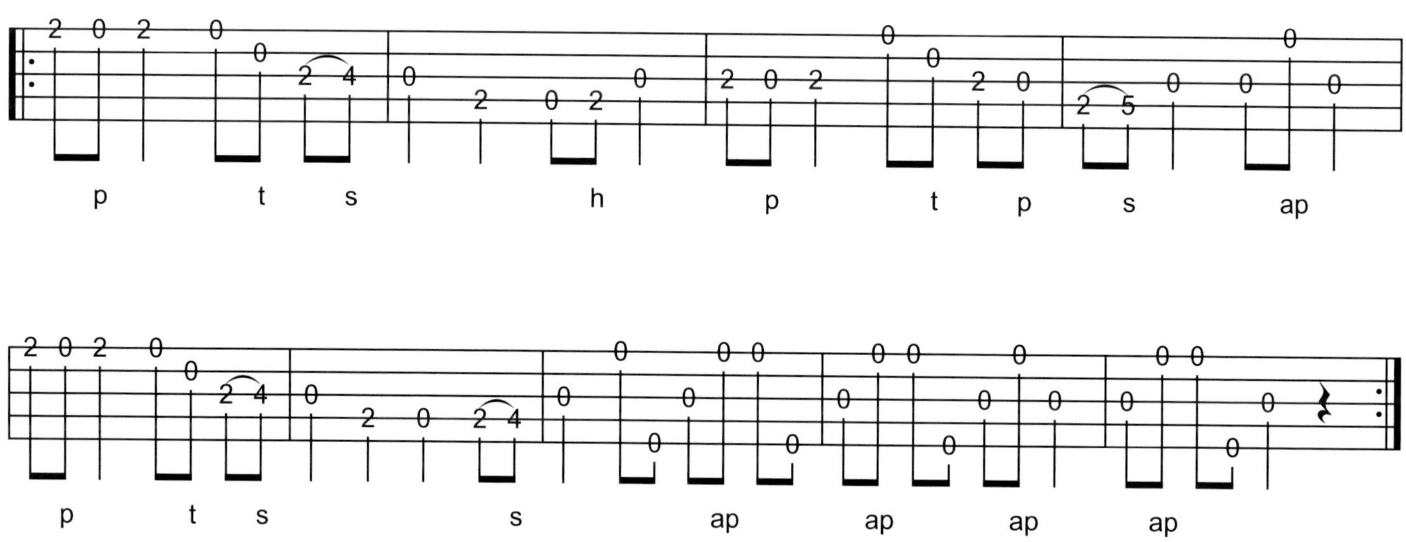

John Henry

as played by Dan

A tuning
aEAC#E (G capo 2)

A part

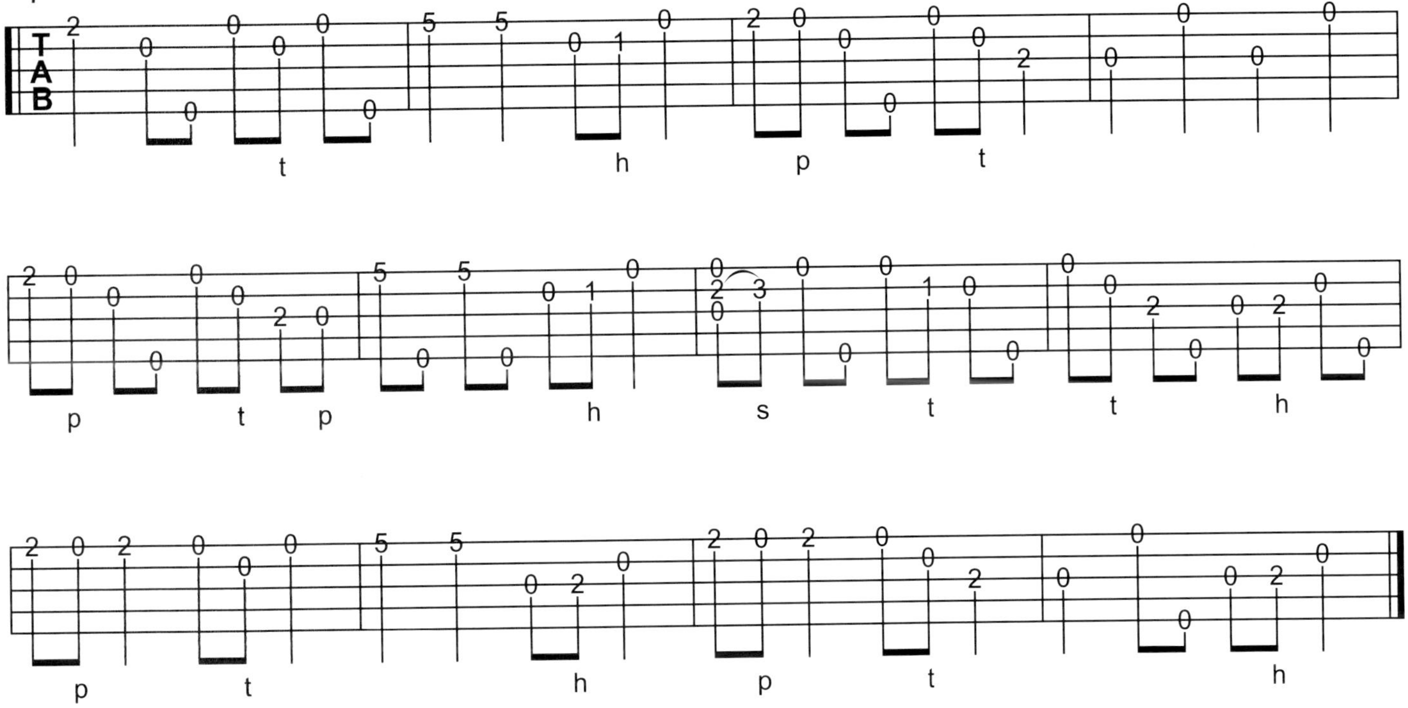

B part

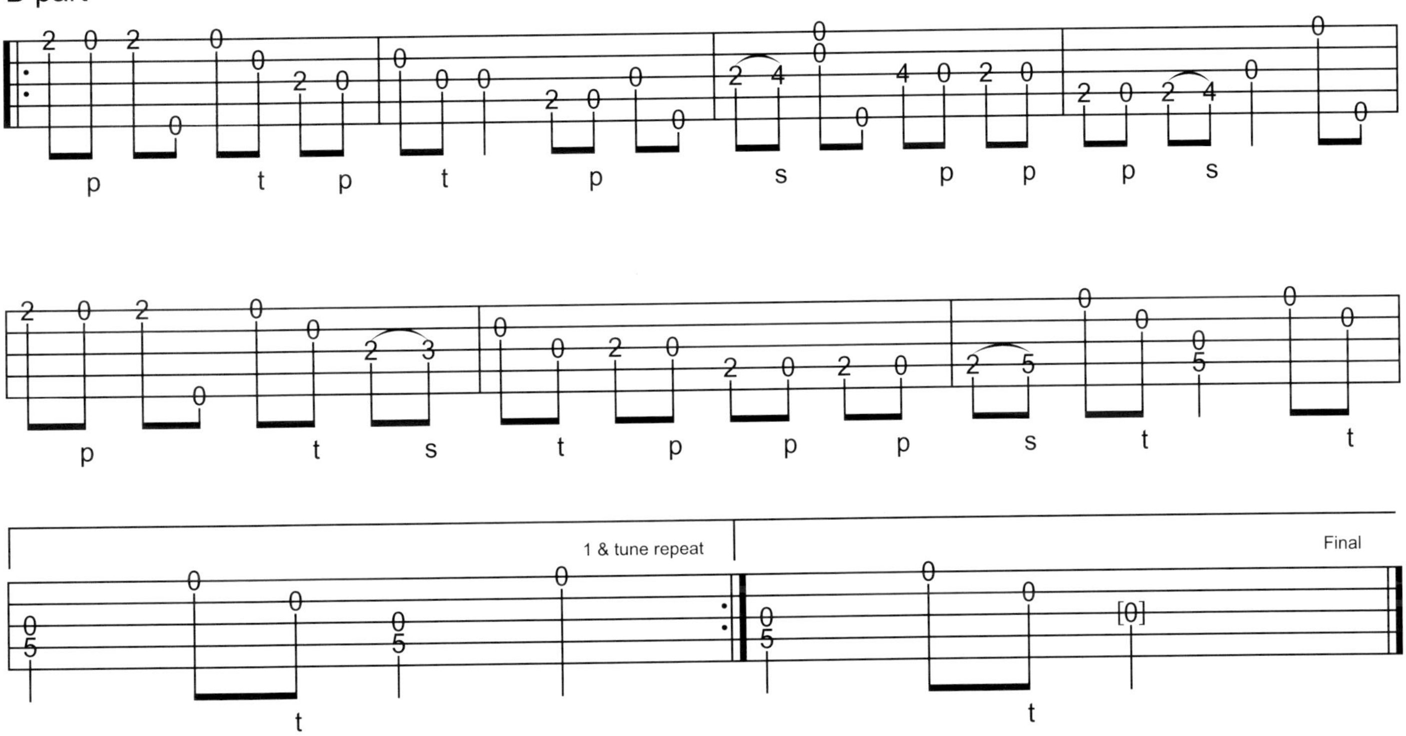

Sometimes Tommy repeats the second (B) part and other times he does not.

Little Maggie

as played by Tommy Jarrell on *Come and Go With Me*

A tuning
aEAC#E (G capo 2)

A part

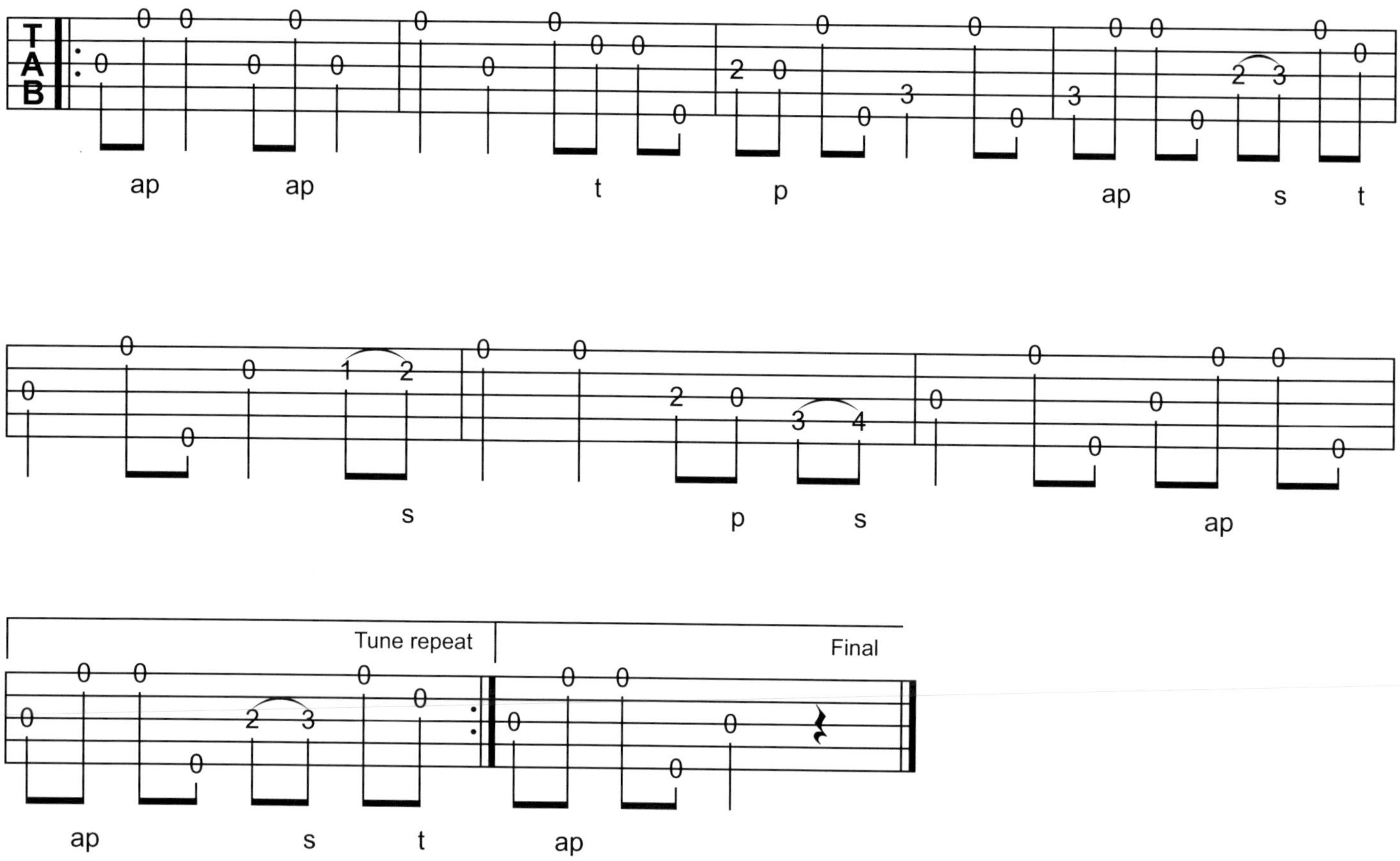

Tommy Jarrell/fiddle and Fred Cockerham/banjo
Photograph by Dave Spilkia
Home of Tommy Jarrell, Toast, NC, August, 1974.

Little Maggie

as played by Dan

A tuning
aEAC#E (G capo 2)

Little Satchel

as played by Fred Cockerham on *Field Recorders Collective*

g#C#F#BE
f#BEAD - capo 2

Fred and Eva Cockerham, probably wedding portrait
Date and photographer unknown

Little Satchel

as played by Dan

g#C#F#BE
f#BEAD - capo 2

I have tabbed my version of the main figure for this tune — the one that follows the words and melody. Fred changes how many times he plays a part or phrase and adds a break that feeds around with a higher melody (see Bob's tab of Fred's playing, previous page) which is something I don't play. It is up to you of course.

The best way to structure this tune for yourself is to listen to Fred play it, see how both of our tabs capture the tune as well as vary from it then go from there to create a good version you feel comfortable playing.

Long Steel Rail

as played by Fred Cockerham on *Clawhammer Banjo Volume 1*

Key of A tuning - aAAC#Eb
(gGGBC# capo 2)

A part

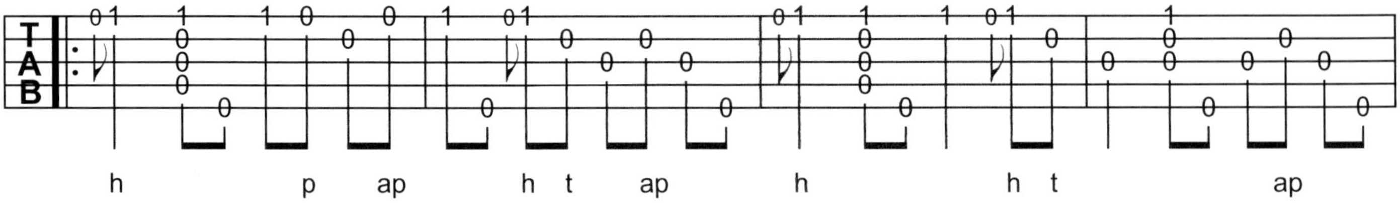

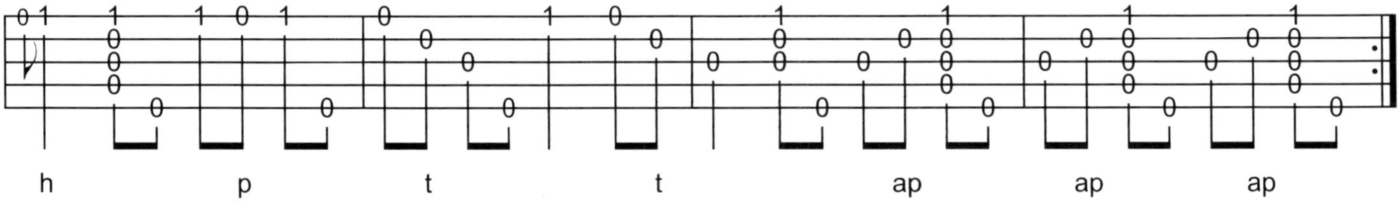

B part

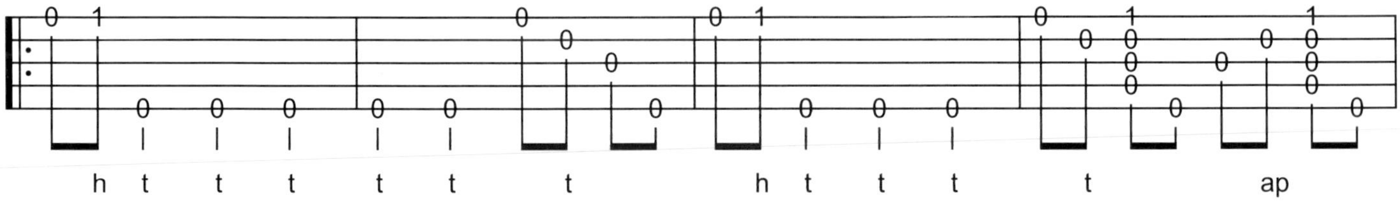

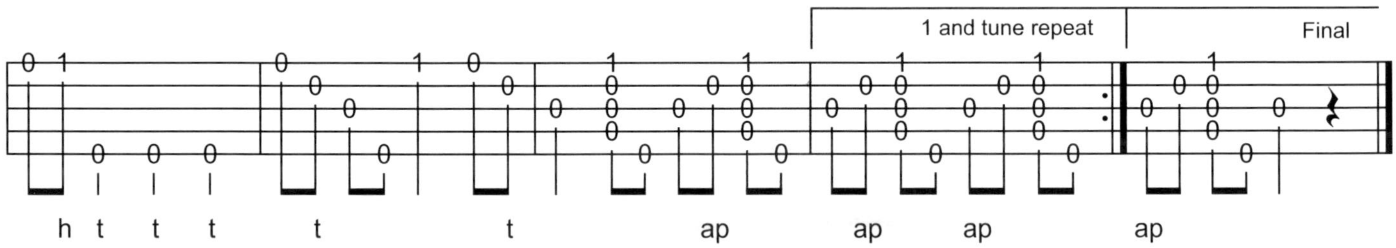

Fred Cockerham/fiddle and Ray Alden/banjo
Photograph by Dave Spilkia
Home of Fred Cockerham, Low Gap, NC, Summer, 1971

Long Steel Rail

as played by Dan

Key of A tuning - aAAC#E
(gGGBC# capo 2)

A part

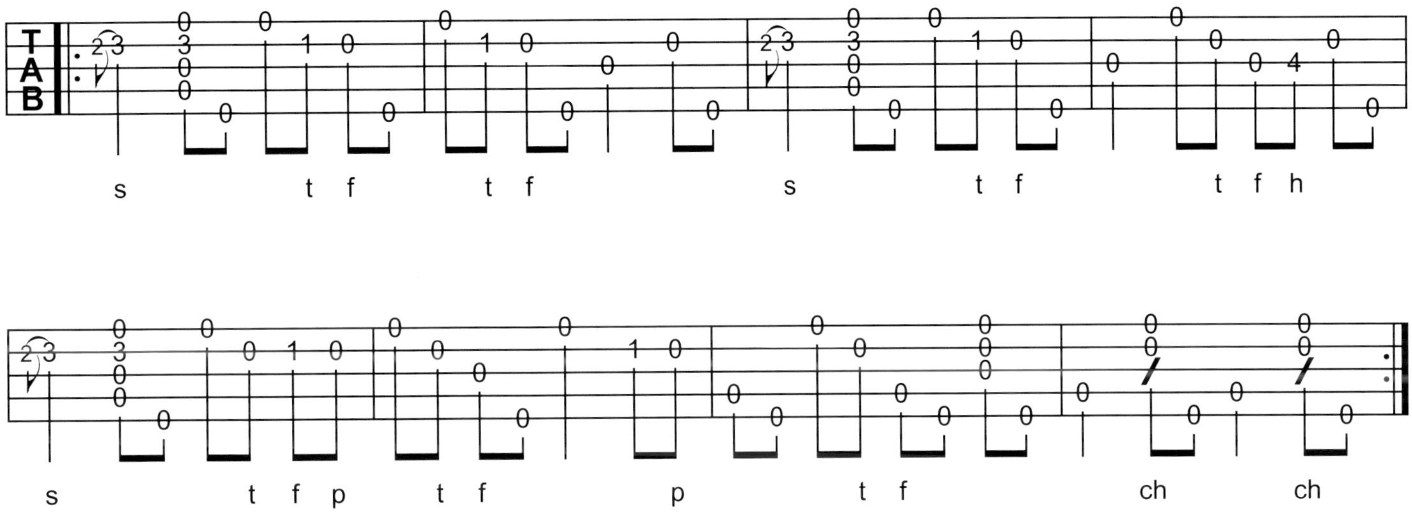

B part

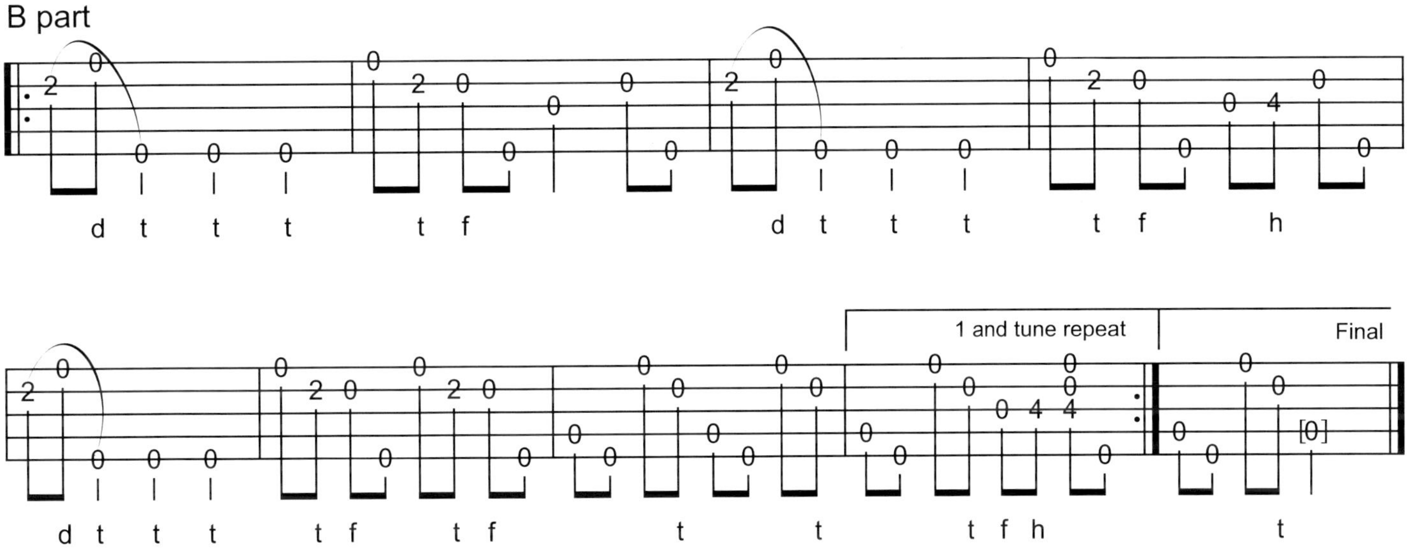

This is another *Reuben* variant. On some private recordings this tune, as well as what is titled *Train 45* in this book are both titled as *Reuben* or *Reuben's Train.* This one shows up as the "alternate" version. The title use here, Long Steel Rail, is how it is titled on the recording Clawhammer Banjo Volume 1 — a *must have* recording for anyone wanting to hear this clawhammer banjo style as it was originally collected.

Also note: I have my first string tuned up to E for my version as opposed to the Eb in Bob's transcription. .

Love Somebody

(aka Soldier's Joy)
as played by Fred Cockerham on *Field Recorders Collective*

Double D tuning
aDADE (double C capo 2)

A part

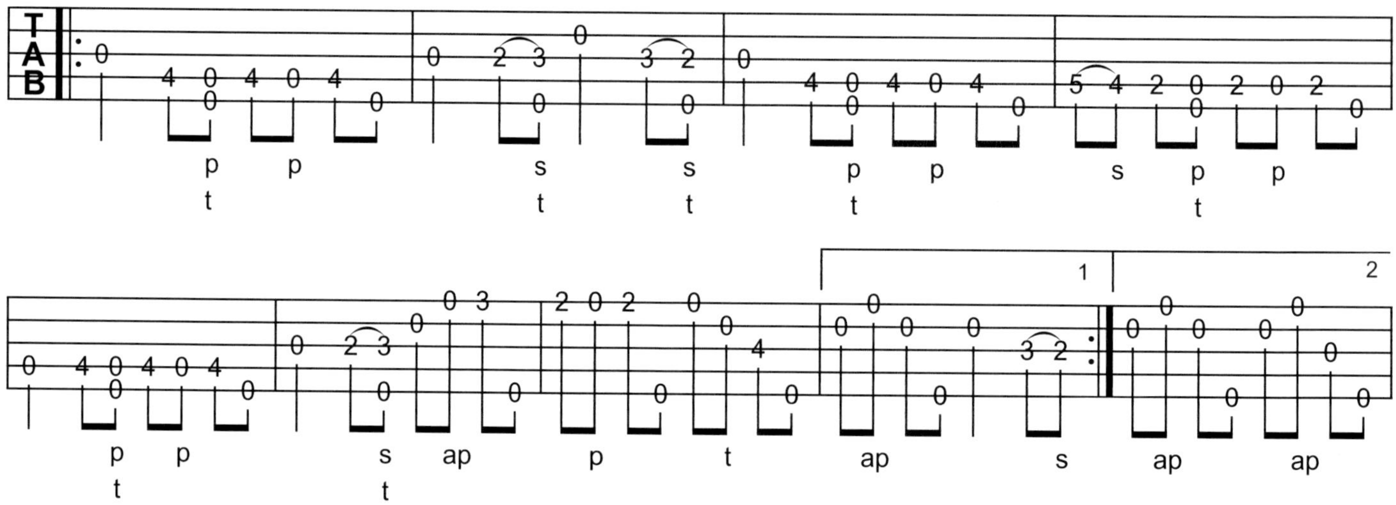

B part

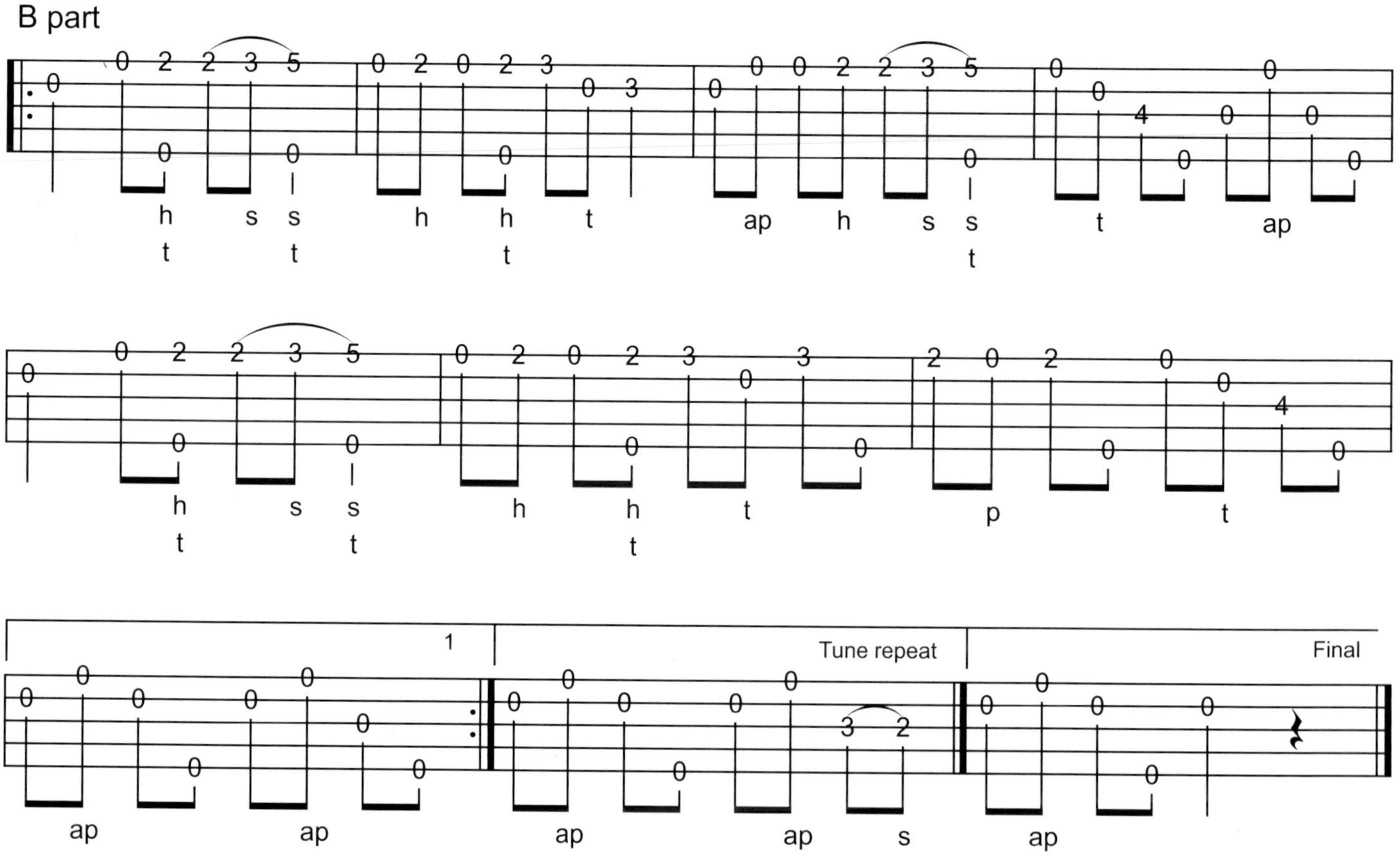

Love Somebody

aka Soldier's Joy
as played by Dan

Double D tuning
aDADE (double C capo 2)

A part

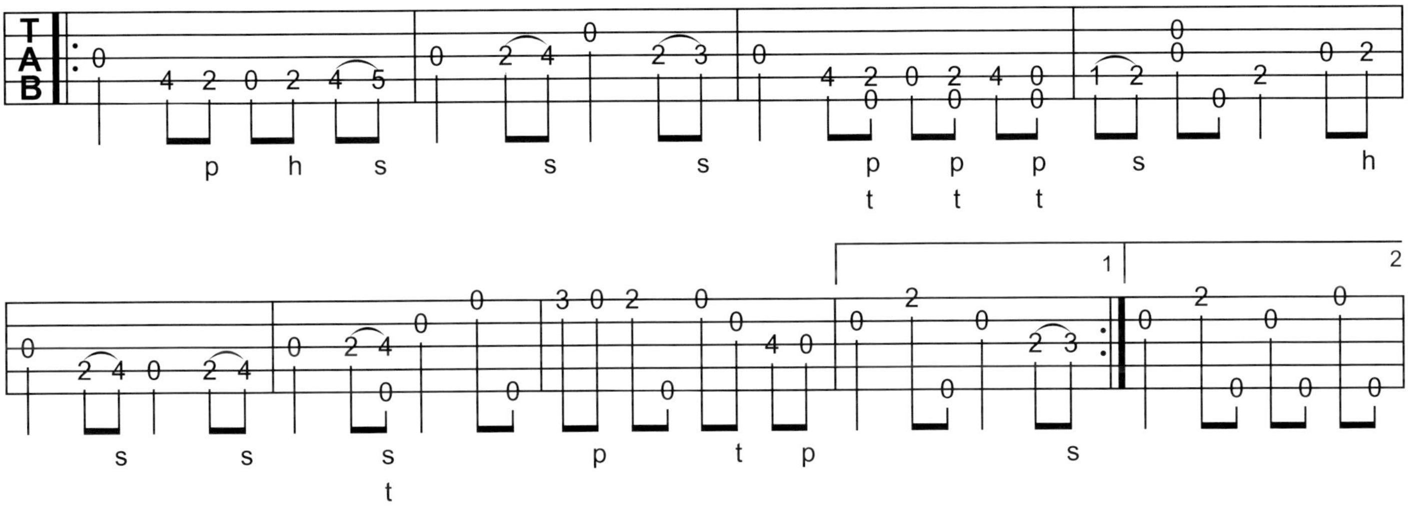

B part

Old Bunch of Keys

as played by Fred Cockerham from the *Field Recorders Collective*

A tuning
aEAC#E (G capo 2)

A part

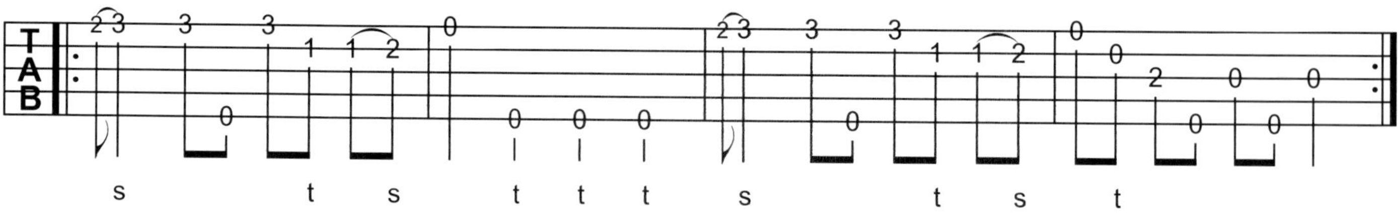

B part

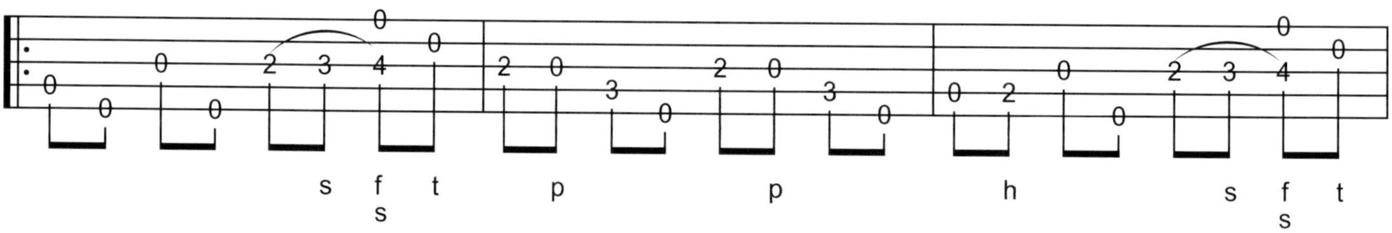

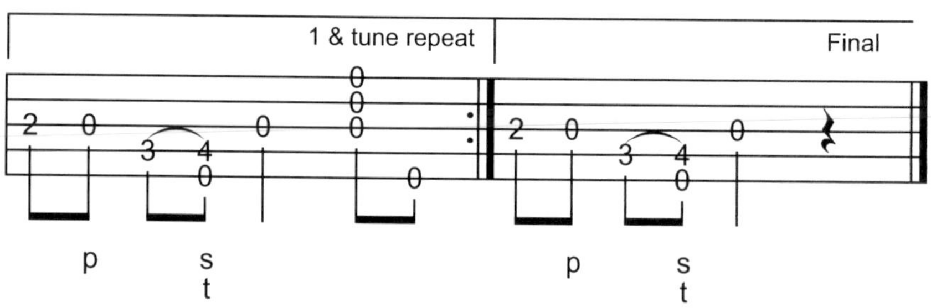

Tommy Jarrell/fiddle and Fred Cockerham/banjo
Photograph by Bill Garbus
Home of Fred Cockerham, Low Gap, NC, Easter, 1972

Old Bunch of Keys

as played by Dan

A tuning
aEAC#E (G capo 2)

A part

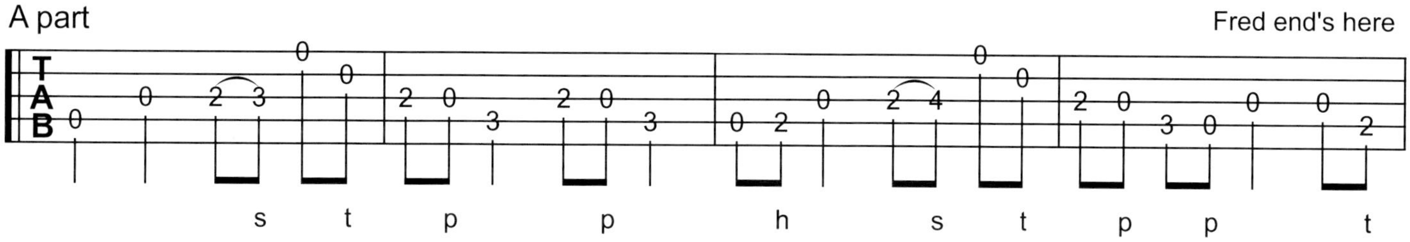

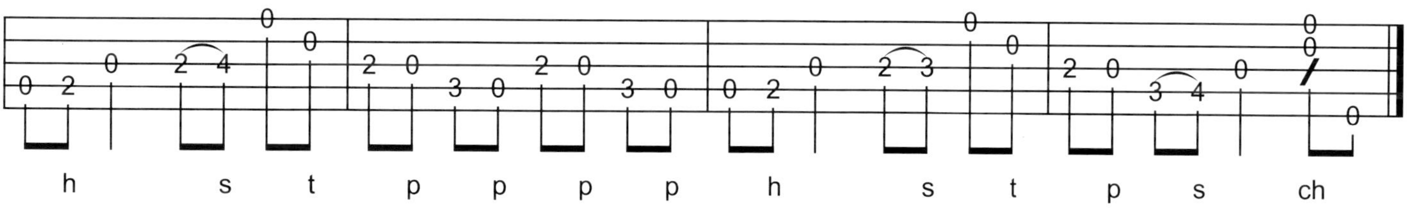

B part

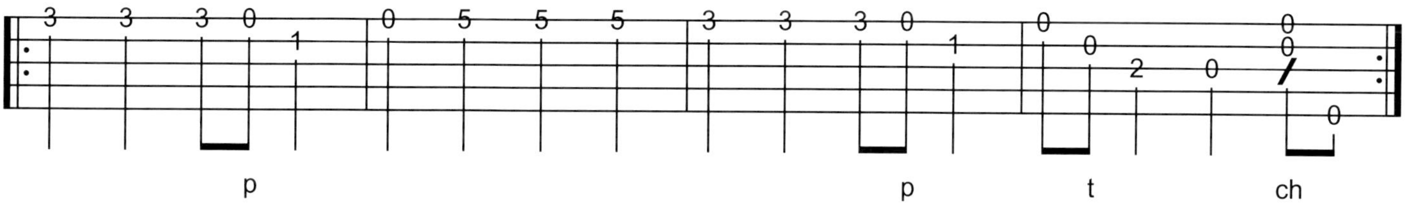

I play the parts here in the order Fred played them on *At Home With Fred* which is how I have always played it. In that recording Fred ends the tune at the end of the first line. Just more evidence that folks didn't just play it one way or even the same way two times through!

I also often repeat the first part and double the second part so I could play it for dances.

Police

as played by Fred Cockerham on *Stay All Night*

A tuning
aEAC#E (G capo 2)

Police

as played by Dan

A tuning
aEAC#E (G capo 2)

Poor Ellen Smith

as played by Tommy Jarrell on *Come and Go With Me*

A tuning
aEAC#E (G capo 2)

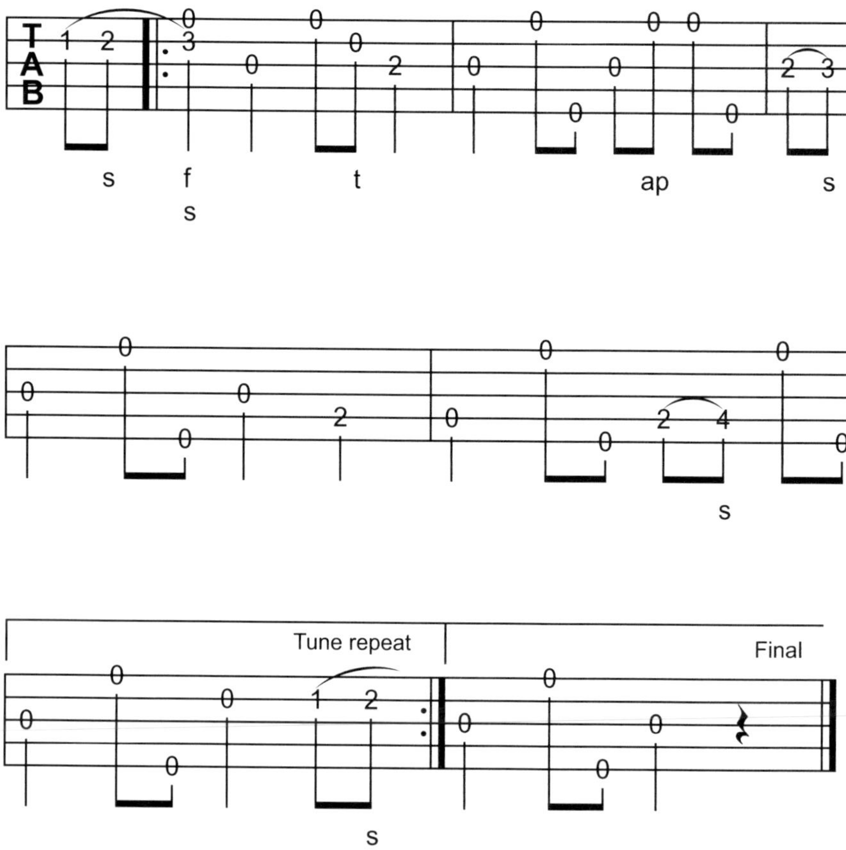

Tommy Jarrell and Fred Cockerham
Photograph by Sandra Stark, location unknown, 1974

Pretty Polly

as played by Dan

A tuning
aEAC#E (G capo 2)

Pretty Polly

as played by Fred Cockerham from the *Field Recorders Collective*

A tuning
aEAC#E (G capo 2)

Pretty Polly

as played by Dan

A tuning
aEAC#E (G capo 2)

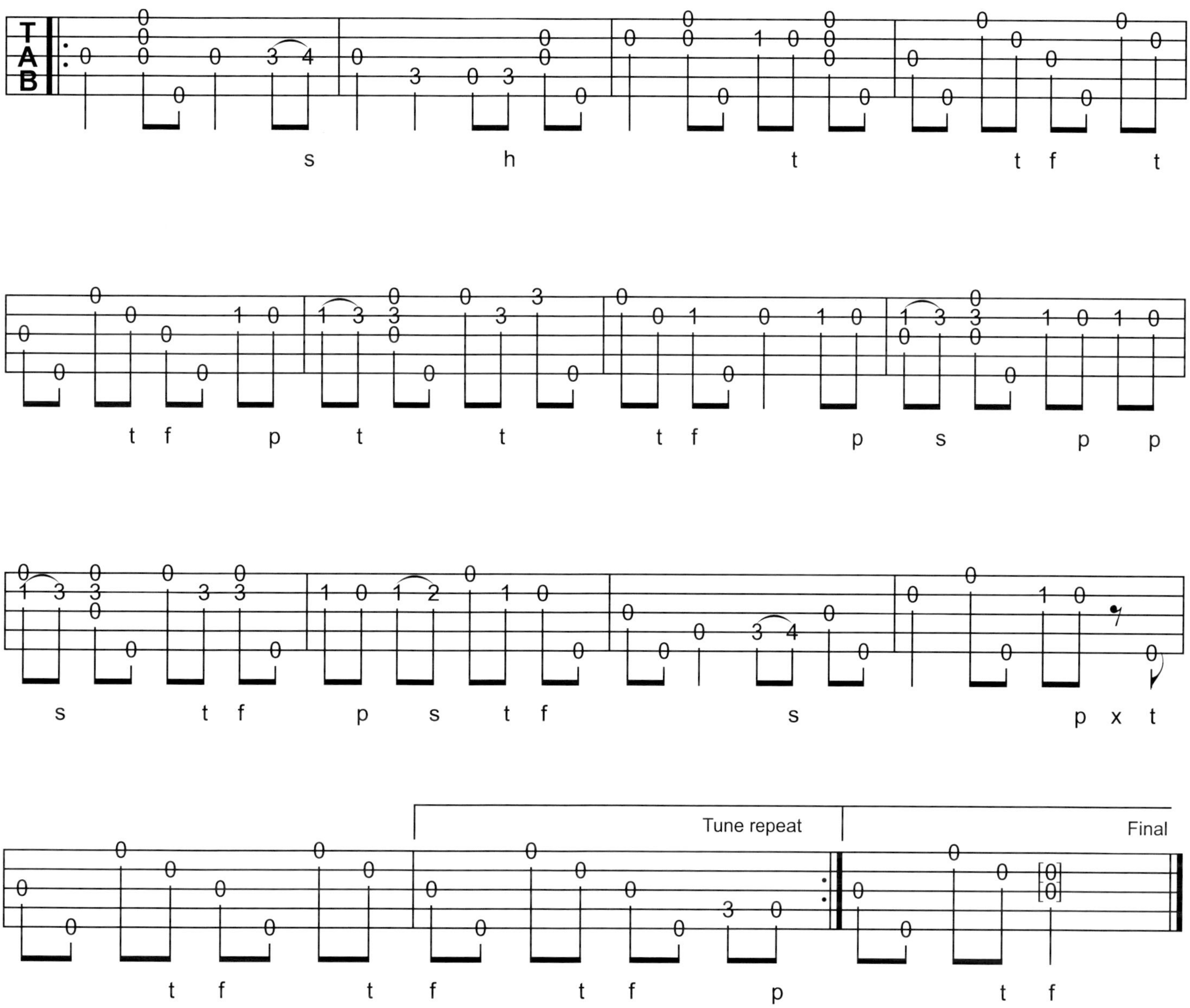

Rockingham Cindy

as played by Tommy Jarrell on *Come and Go With Me*

Double D tuning
aDADE (double C capo 2)

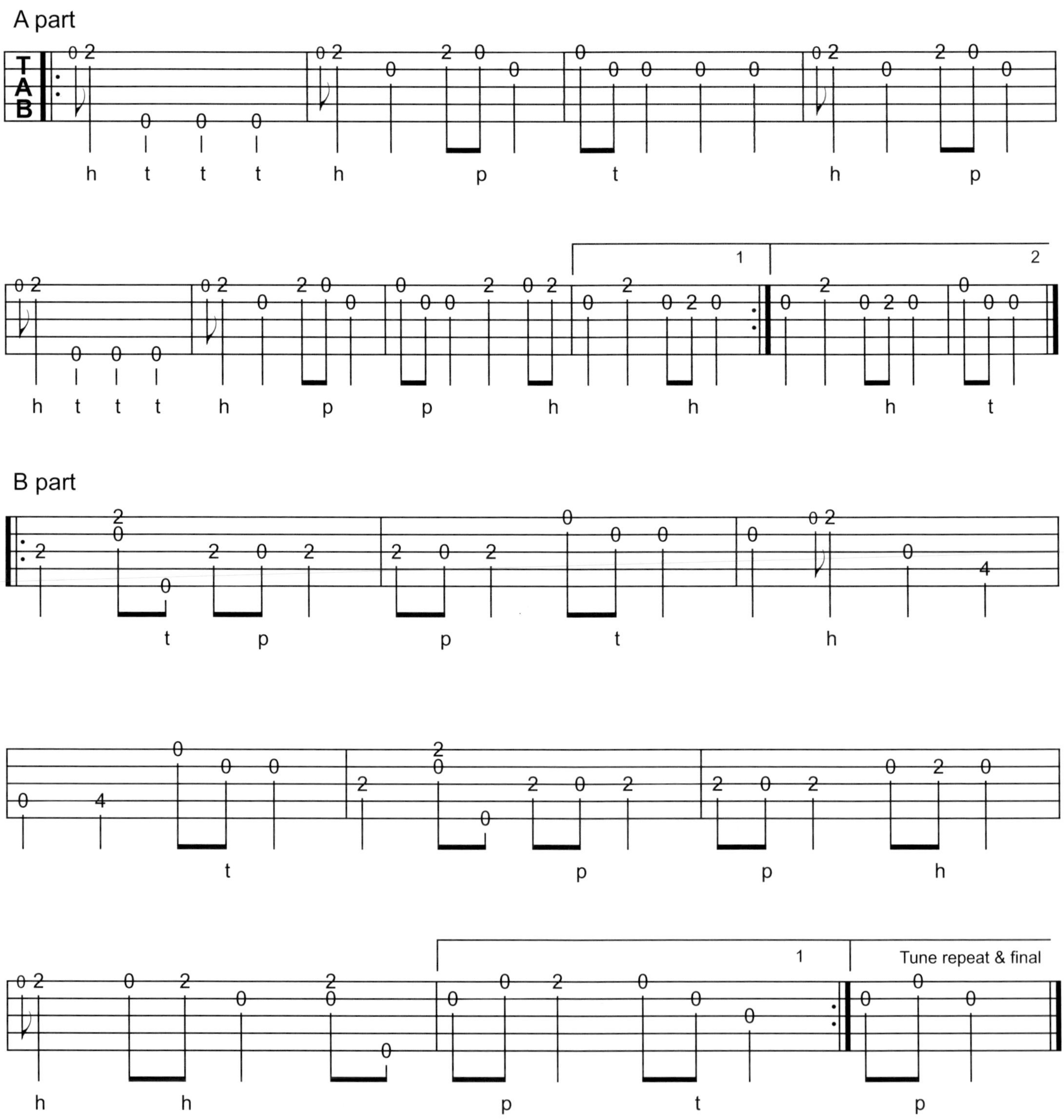

Rockingham Cindy

as played by Dan

Double D tuning
aDADE (double C capo 2)

A part

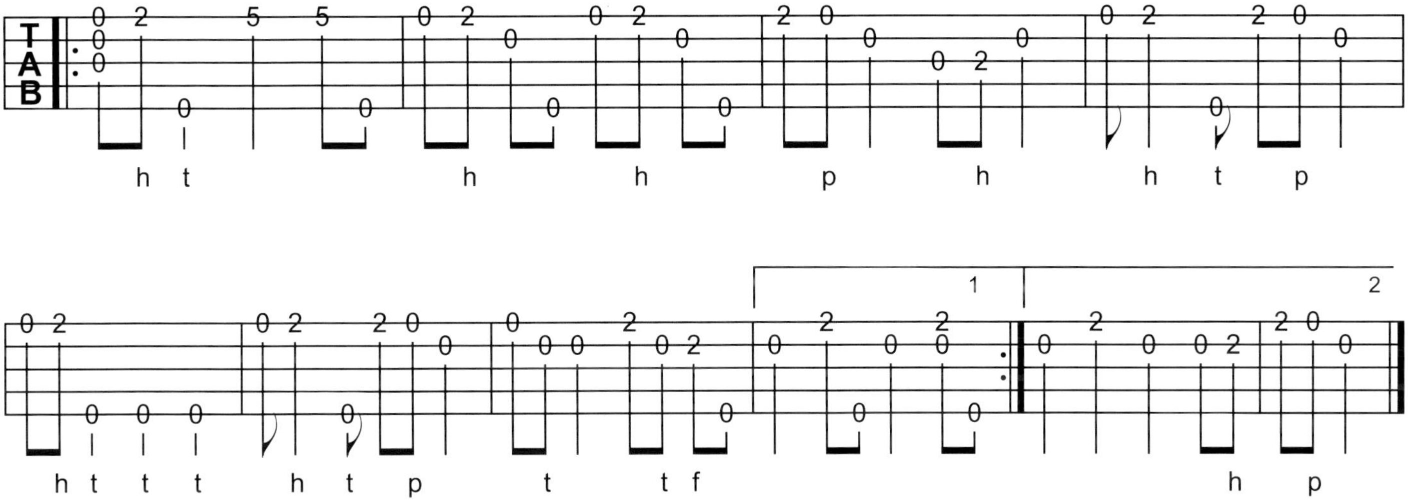

B part

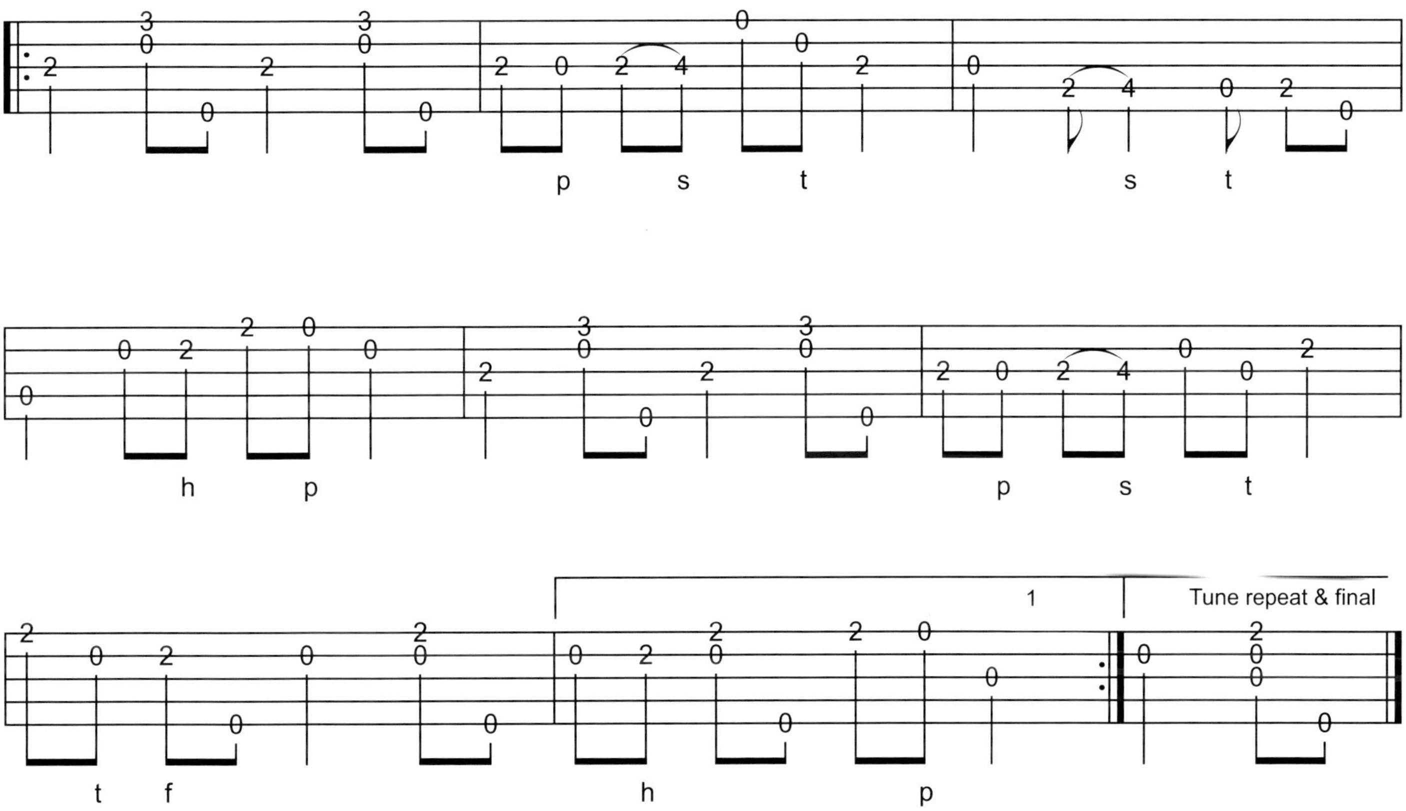

Roustabout

as played by Fred Cockerham on *Clawhammer Banjo Volume 2*

Tuning - aDAC#E
(gCGBD - capo 2)

A part

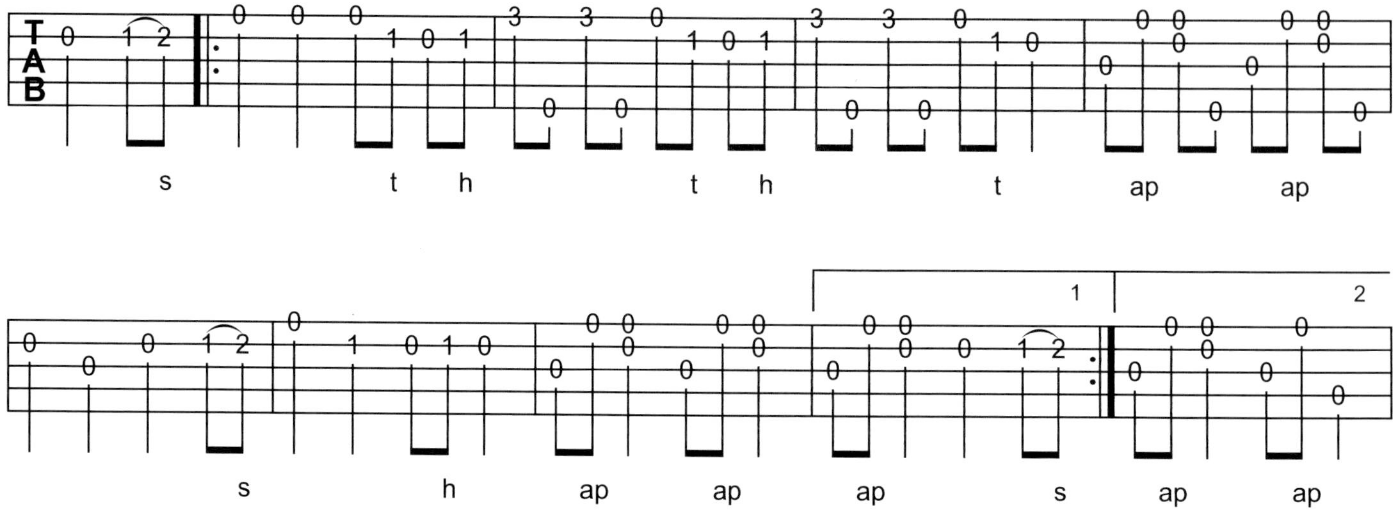

B part

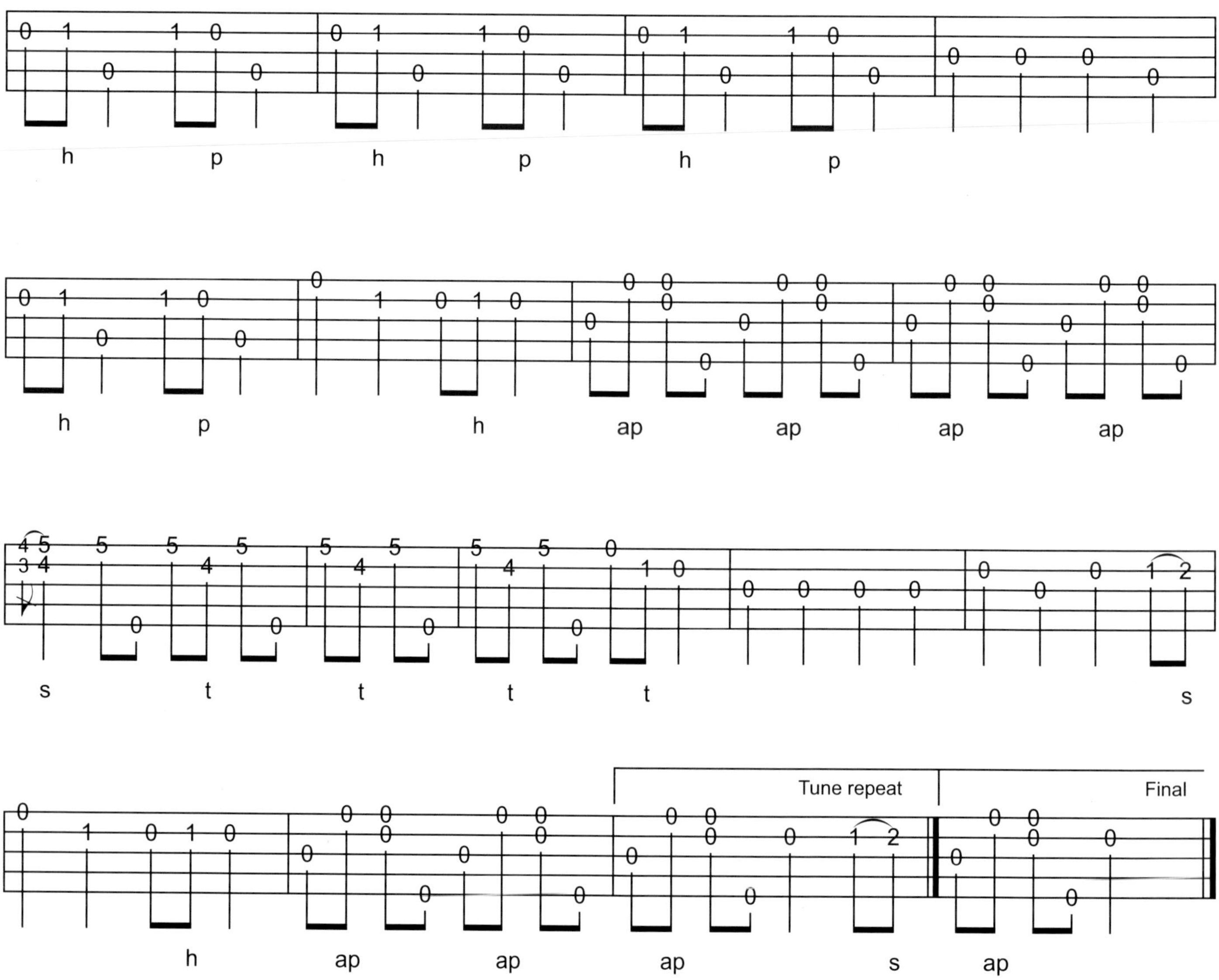

Roustabout

as played by Dan

Tuning - aDAC#E
(gCGBD - capo 2)

A part

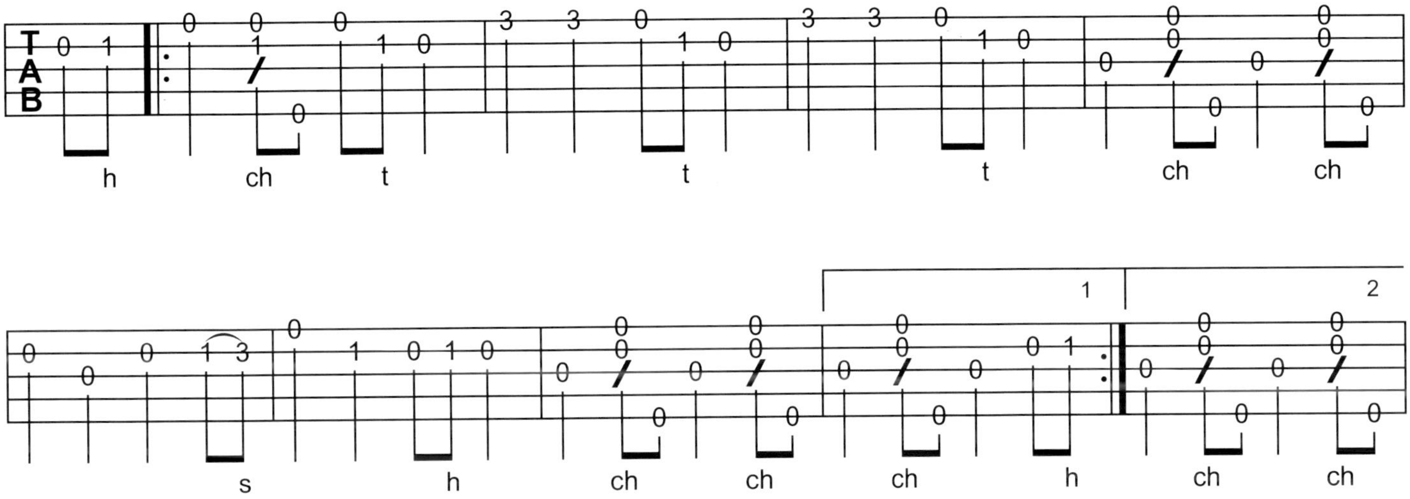

B part

Stay All Night

as played by Fred Cockerham on *Stay All Night*

A tuning
aEAC#E (G capo 2)

A part

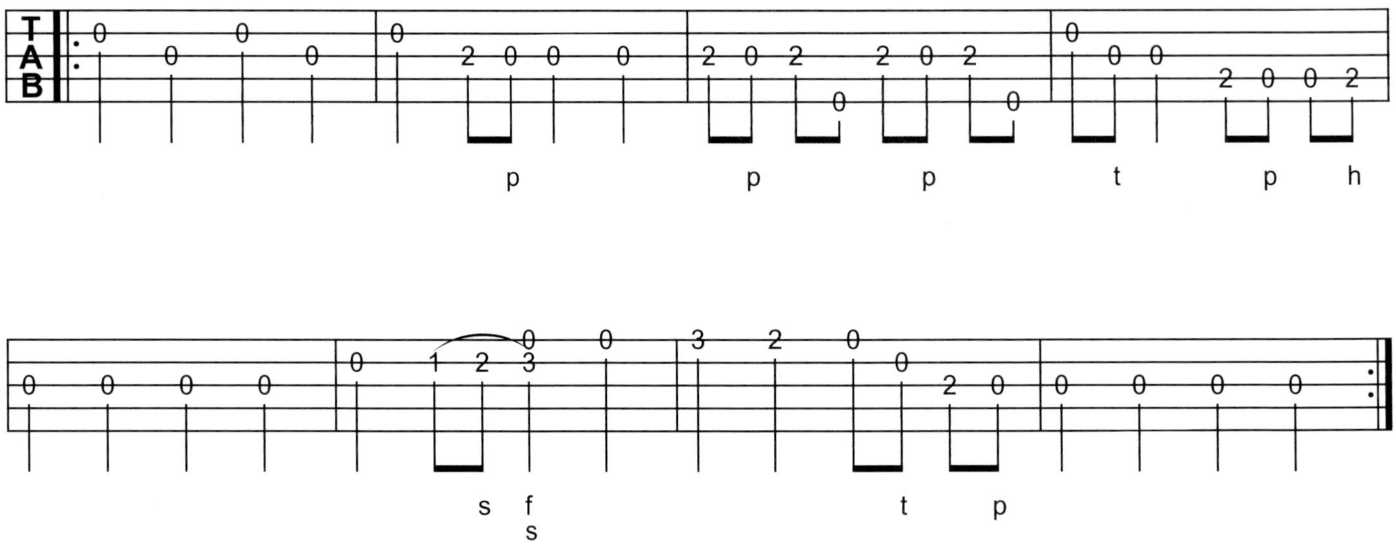

B part

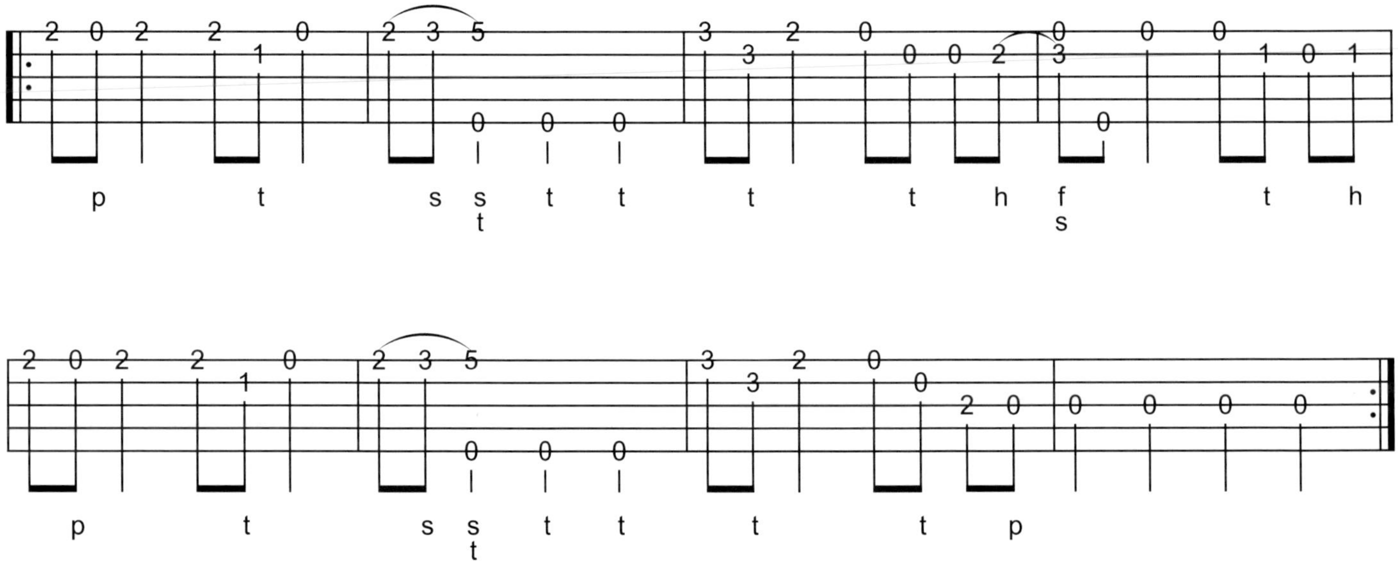

Stay All Night

as played by Dan

A tuning
aEAC#E (G capo 2)

A part

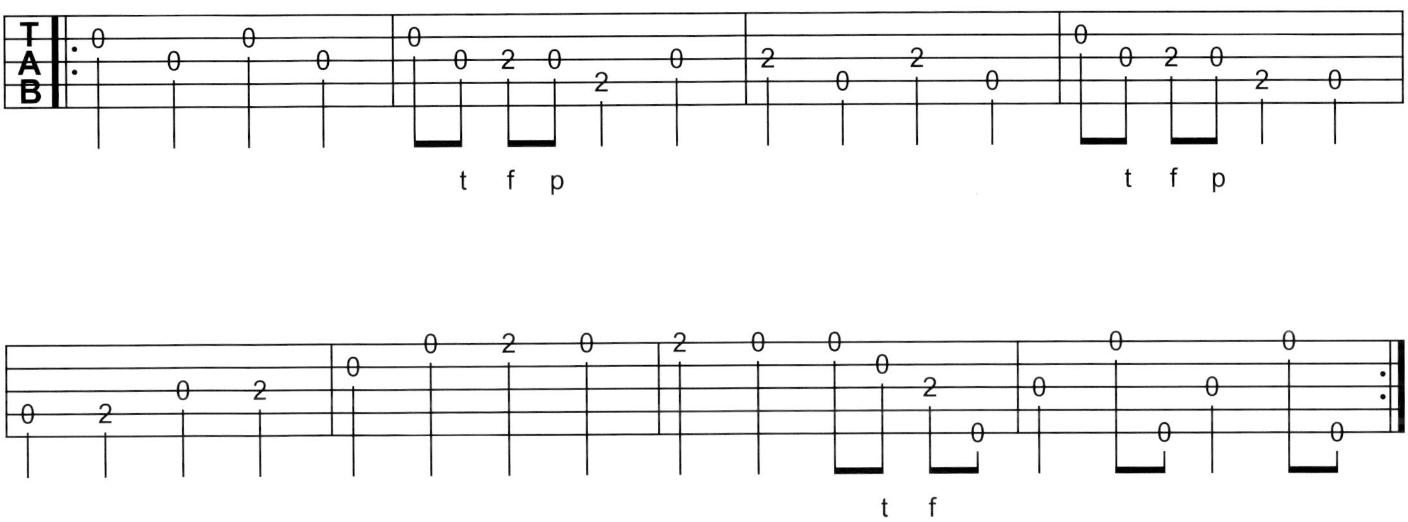

B part

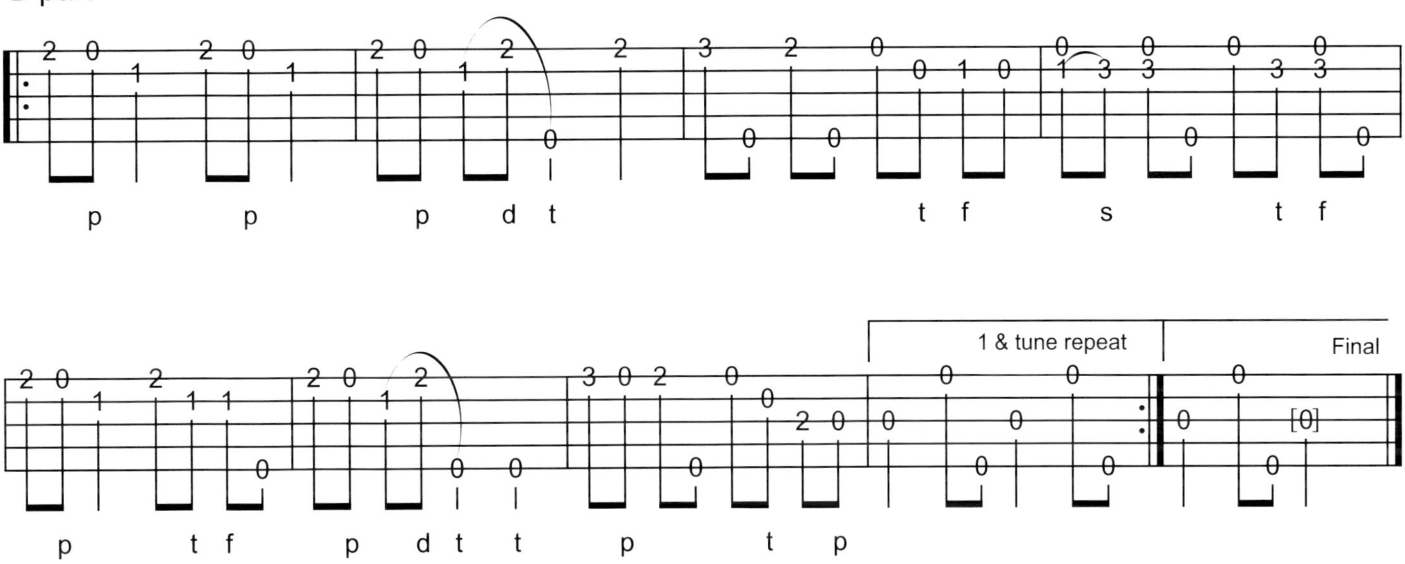

Sweet Sunny South

as played by Tommy Jarrell on *Come and Go With Me*

A tuning
aEAC#E (G capo 2)

Sweet Sunny South

as played by Dan

A tuning
aEAC#E (G capo 2)

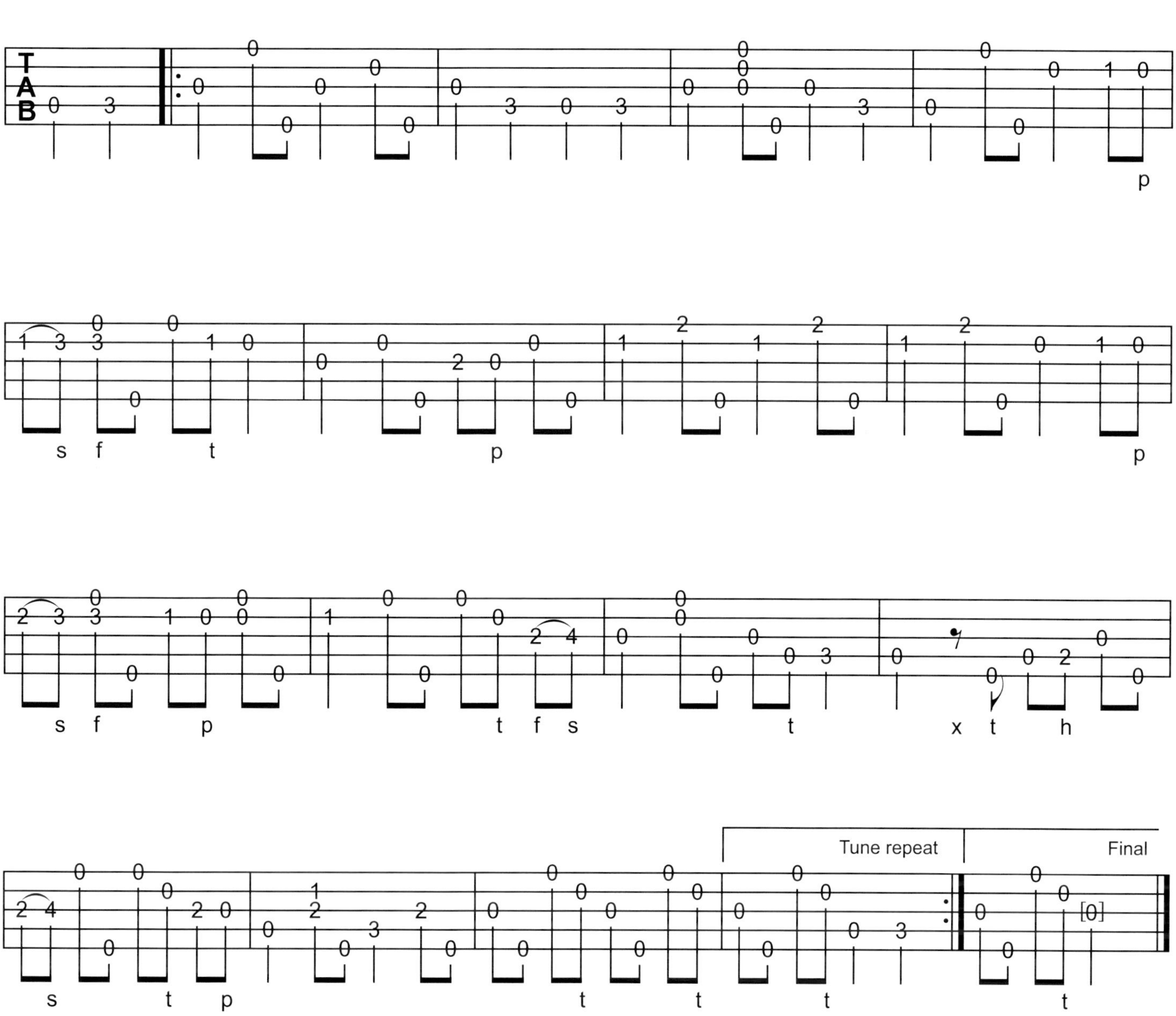

Tempie

as played by Tommy Jarrell on *Come and Go With Me*

Double D tuning
aDADE (double C capo 2)

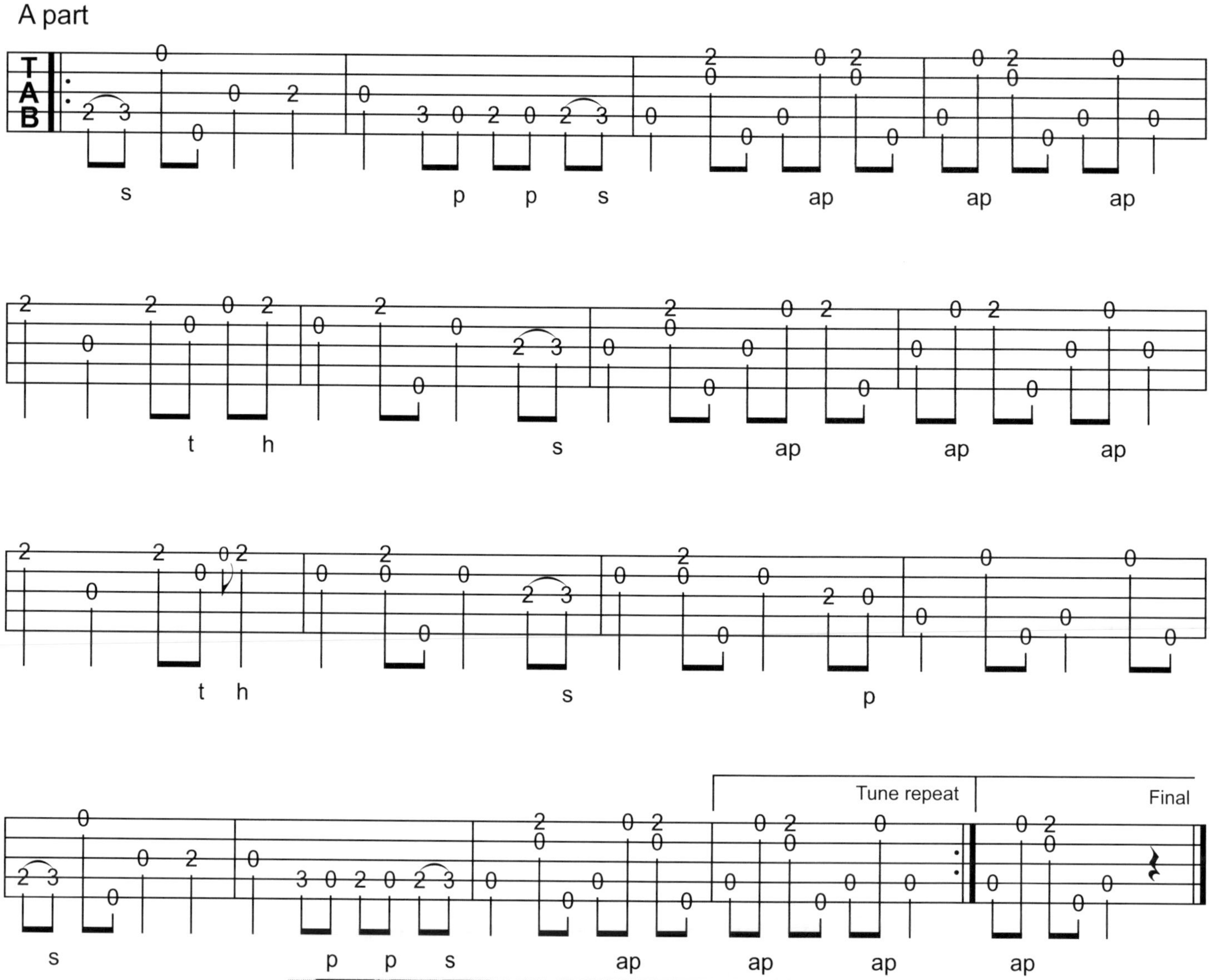

Tommy Jarrell/fiddle and Fred Cockerham/banjo
Photograph by Bill Garbus
Home of Fred Cockerham, Low Gap, NC, Easter, 1972

Tempie

as played by Dan

Double D tuning
aDADE (double C capo 2)

A part

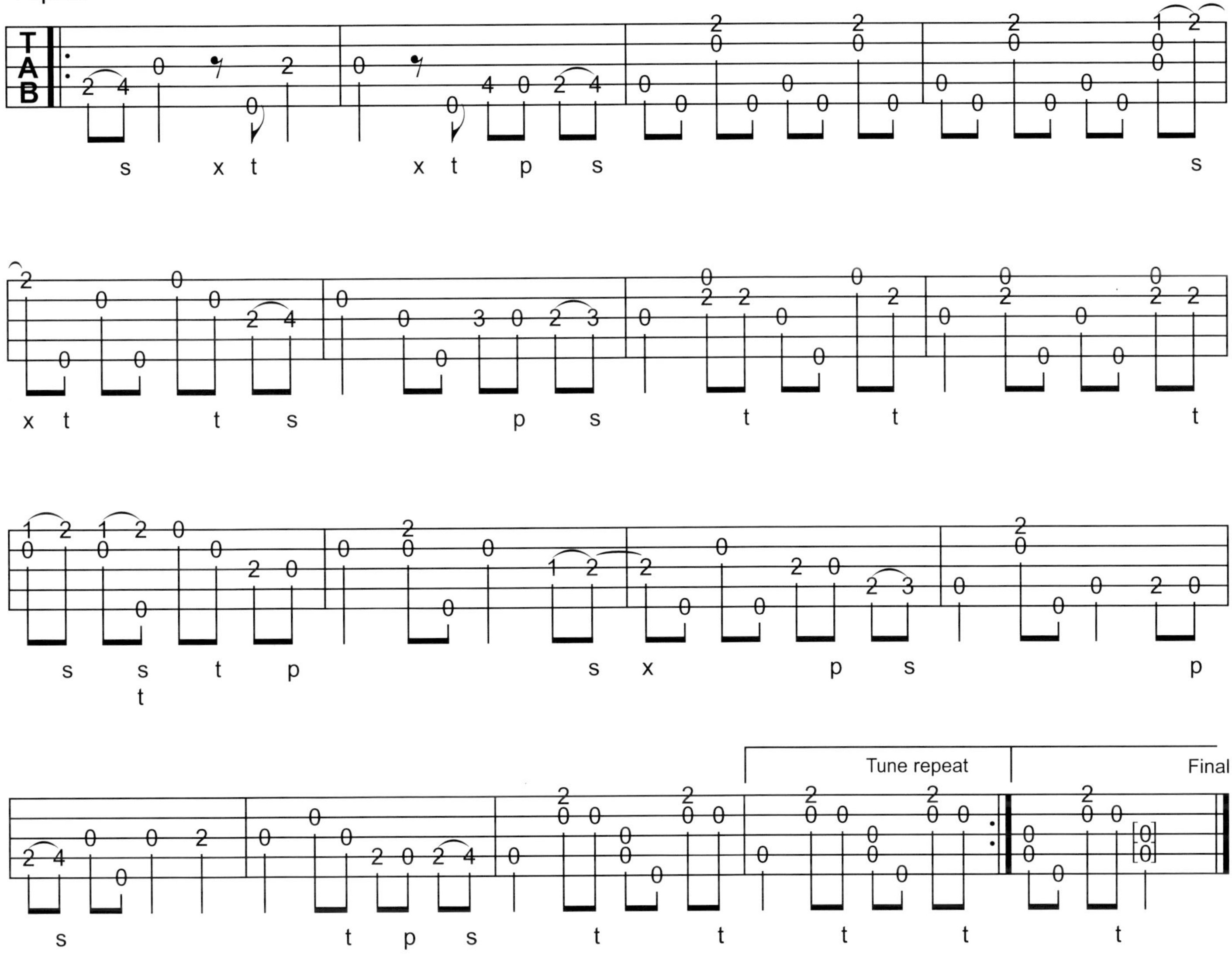

Train 45 aka Reuben or Reuben's Train

as played by Fred Cockerham on *Field Recorders Collective*

A tuning
aEAC#E (G capo 2)

A part

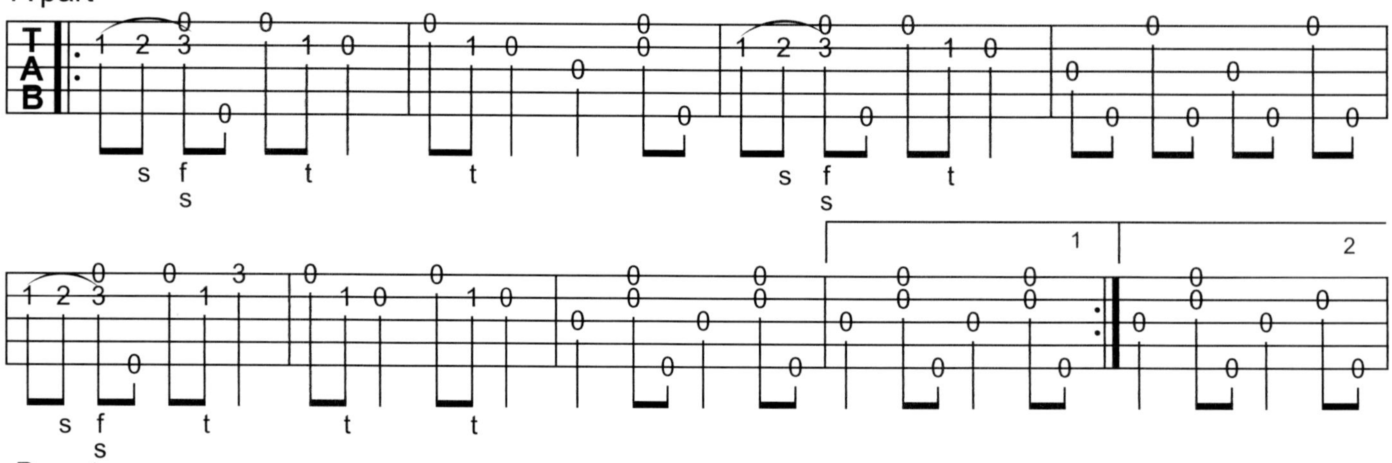

B part

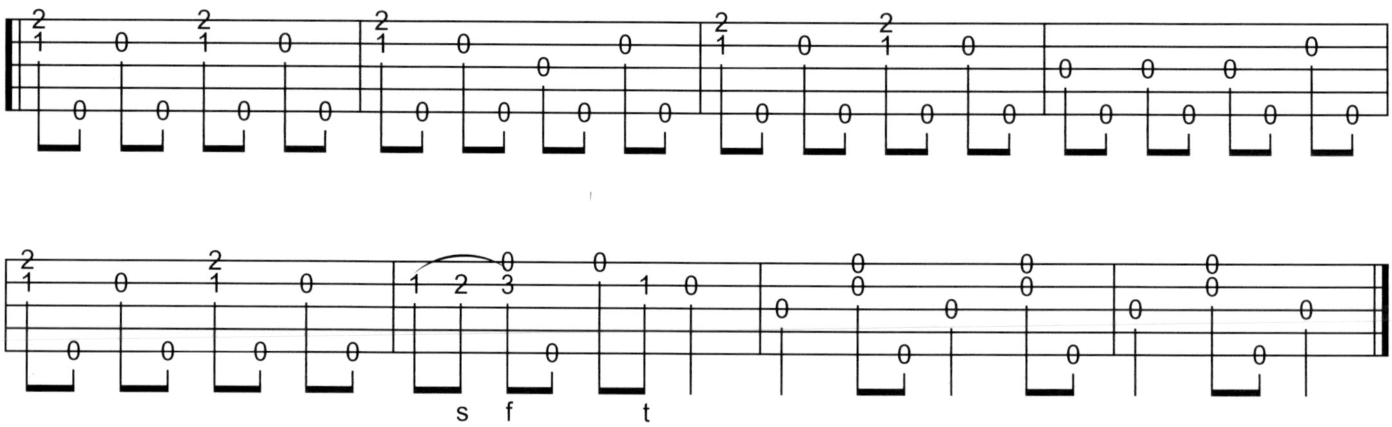

C part

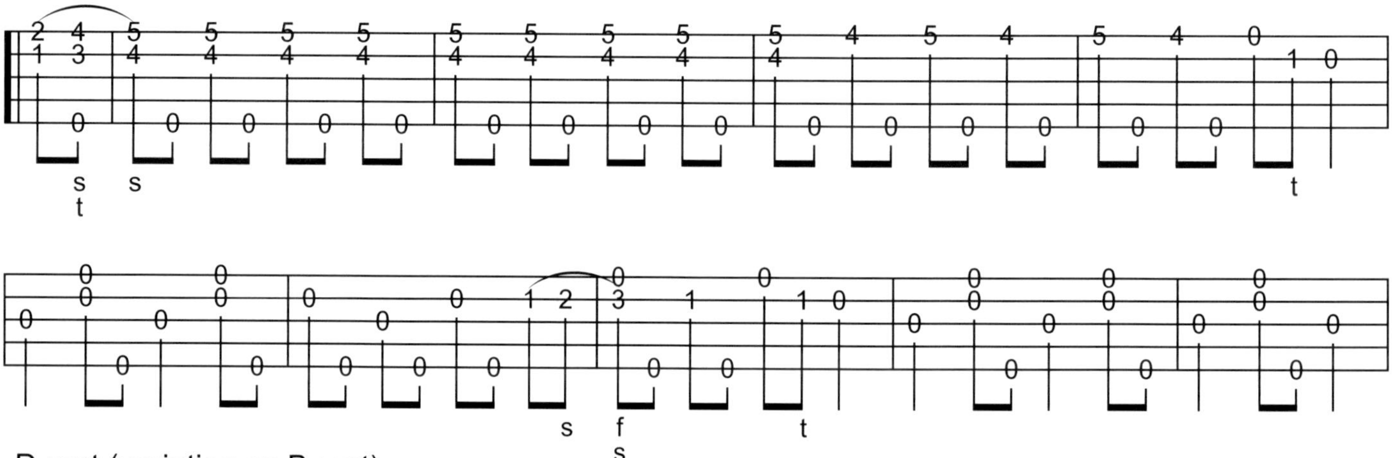

D part (variation on B part)

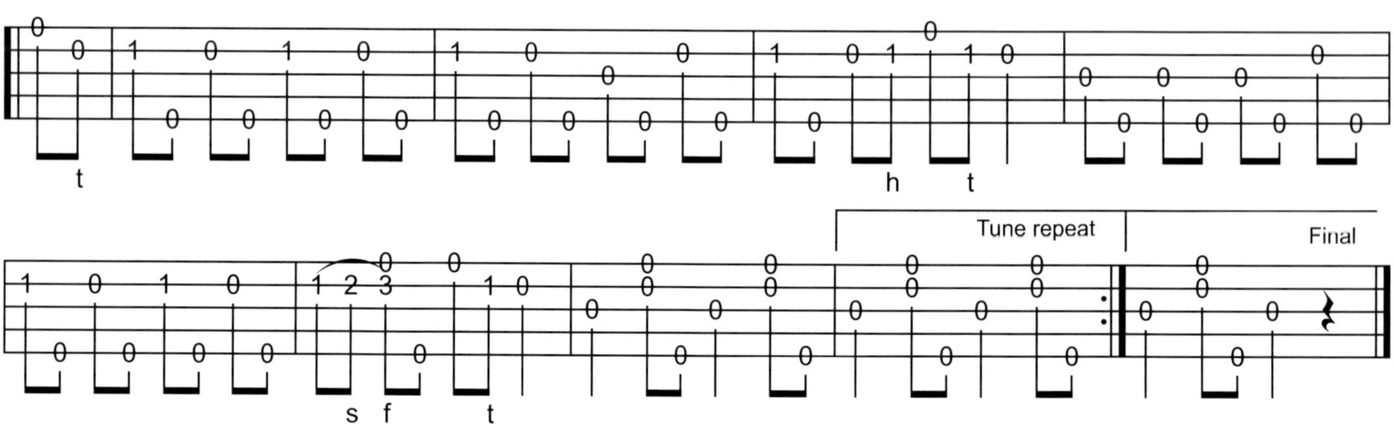

Train 45 aka Reuben or Reuben's Train

A tuning
aEAC#E (G capo 2)

as played by Dan

A part

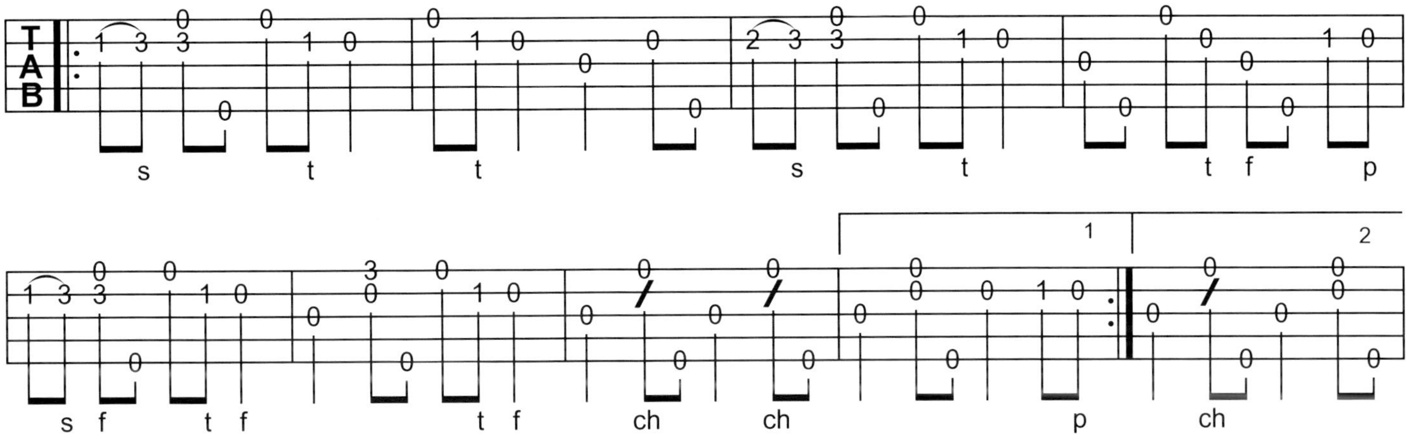

B part

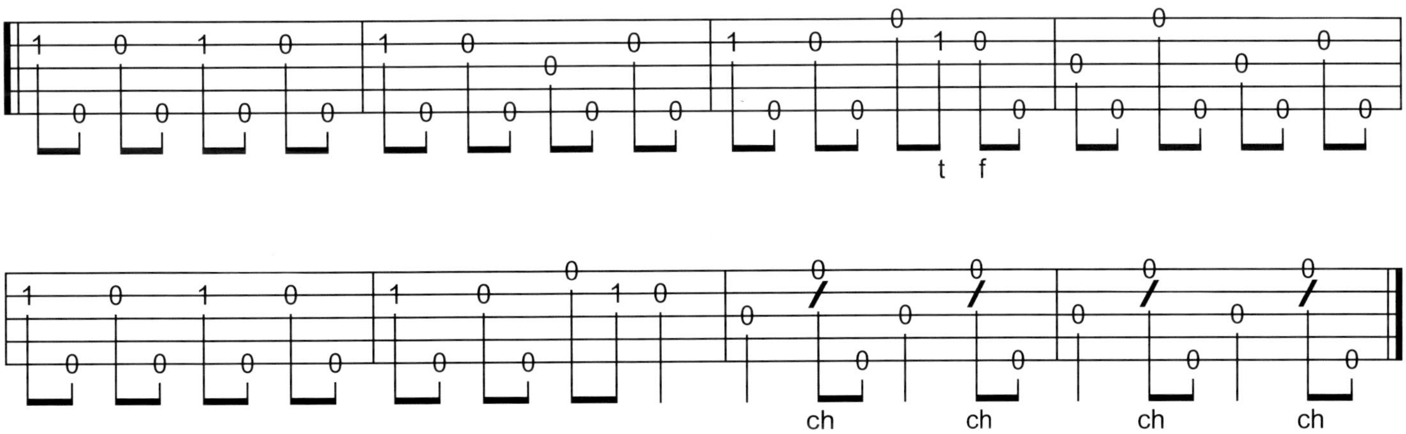

C part

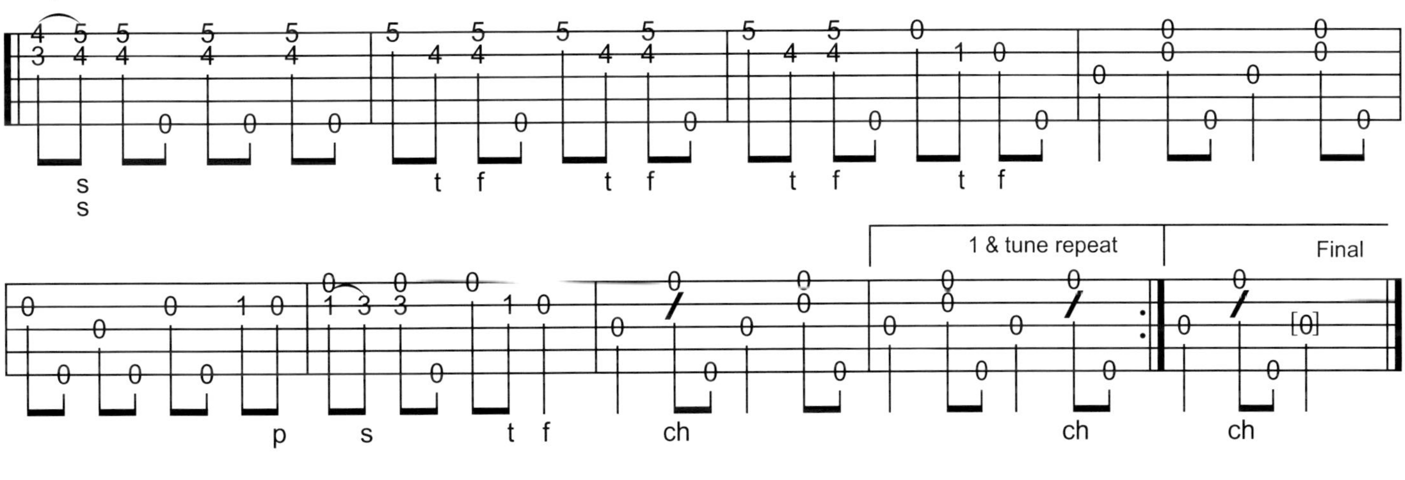

I have only written 3 parts here because as Bob notes in his D part, it is basically a variation of the B part. I also have straightened the tune out as Fred sometimes did.

Also, Fred was not always consistent in the number of times he plays a part or how many parts he plays from one time to the next.

See the note on page 31 for more about this tune's name.

Yellow Rose of Texas

as played by Fred Cockerham on *Tommy and Fred*

Double D tuning
aDADE (double C capo 2)

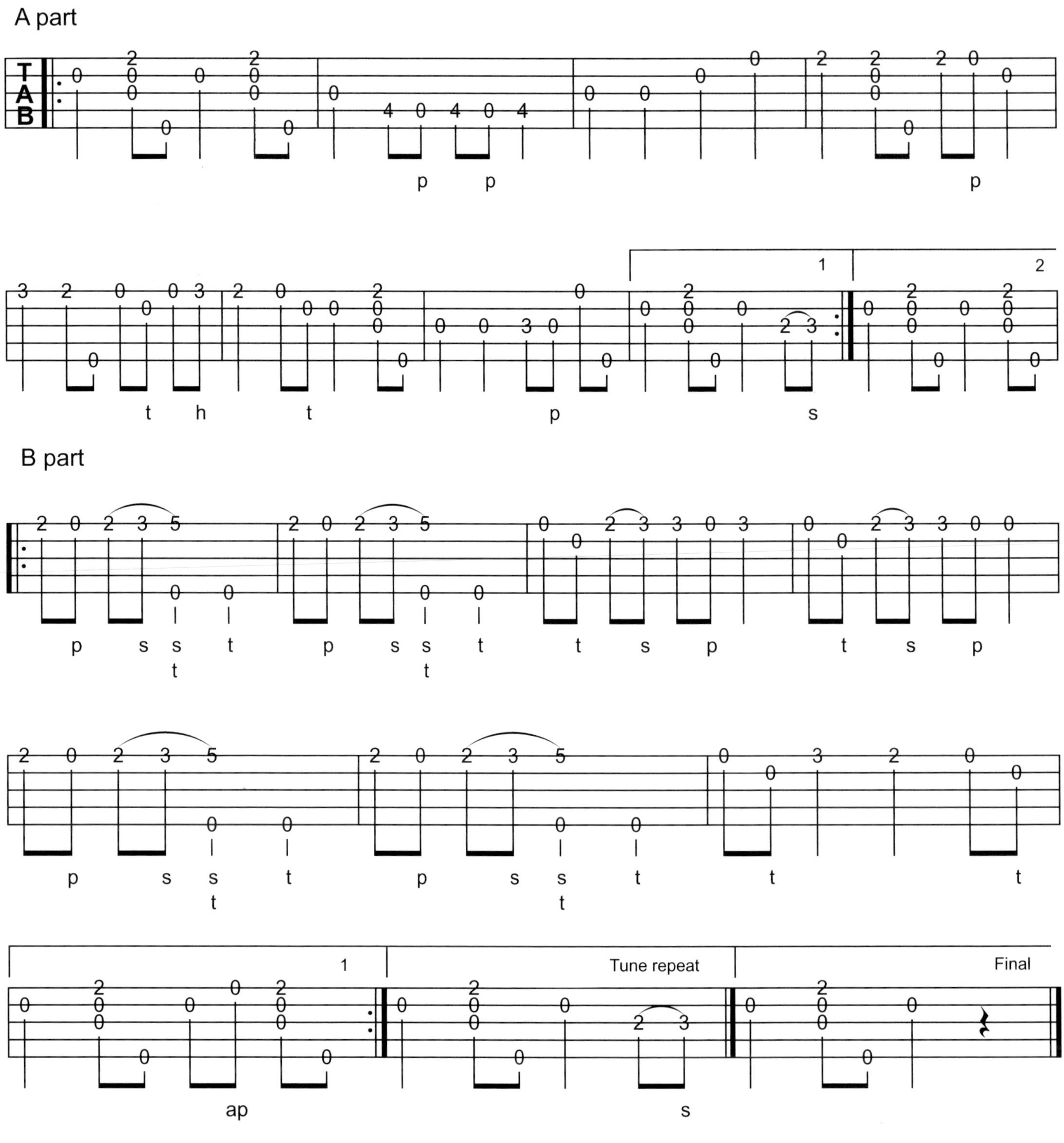

Yellow Rose of Texas

as played by Dan

Double D tuning
aDADE (double C capo 2)

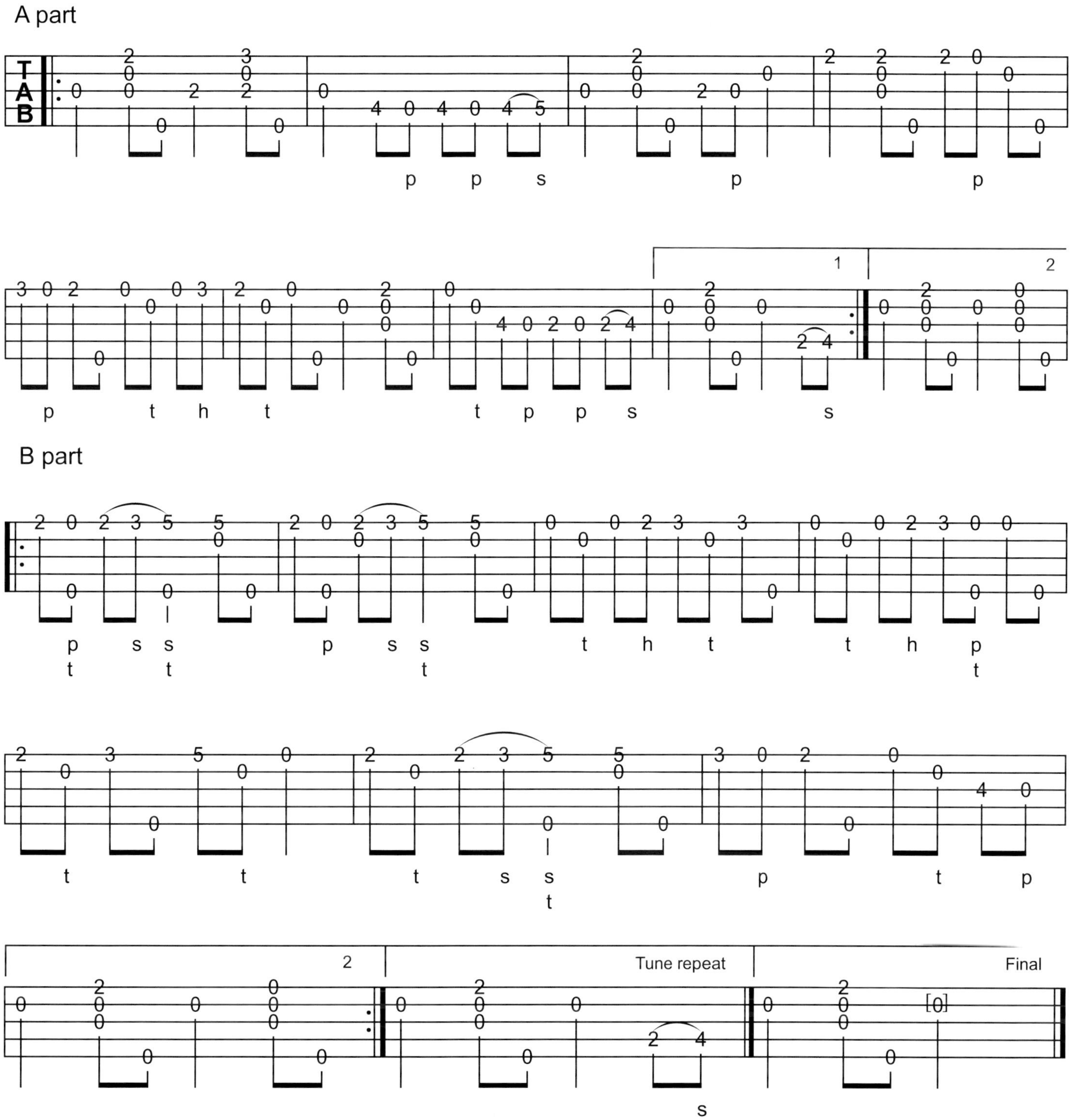

Dan Levenson is a Southern Appalachian native who has grown up with the music of that region. Today he is considered to be a master teacher and performer of both the Clawhammer banjo & the Southern Appalachian fiddle style.

Dan has won awards on both instruments including first place at the 2005 Ohio Clawhammer Banjo Championship and Grand Champion at the 2010 Ajo, AZ fiddle contest. He has over 10 recordings both with his band *The Boiled Buzzards* and as a solo artist. Dan performs and teaches regularly throughout the country. He has taught at many of the traditional music schools and camps including the *John C. Campbell Folk School, Mars Hill, Maryland Banjo Academy, The Ozark Folk Center* at Mountain View, AR and *Banjo Camp North.* He currently also runs various clawhammer banjo, fiddle & stringband workshops as well as his innovative *Clawcamp* throughout the year.

Dan is the Mel Bay author of *Clawhammer Banjo From Scratch, Buzzard Banjo Clawhammer Style, Old Time Festival Tunes for Clawhammer Banjo* (a Fiddle & mandolin version also available)*, Gospel Tunes for Clawhammer Banjo, Kyle Creed Clawhammer Banjo Master, Wade Ward Clawhammer Banjo Master,* and *Old Time Favorites for Clawhammer Banjo* (a Fiddle & mandolin version is also available) . He has written for *The Old Time Herald* and is a writer and editor for *Banjo Newsletter's Old Time Way.*

For Dan's books, recordings and more information about Dan, please go to *www.Clawdan.com*

Bob Carlin is probably the best known clawhammer style banjoist performing today. Faithful to timeless Southern Traditions, he has taken the distinctive southern banjo style to appreciative audiences all over the US, Canada, Europe, Australia and Japan. As a solo performer, and a member of John Hartford's Stringband, Bob has appeared at countless festivals, clubs, schools and museums. Carlin is a three-time winner of the Frets Magazine reader's poll, and has four Rounder albums to his credit.

Bob Carlin has studied both in person and on transcriptions the work of master players from previous generations. Along with researching several books and countless articles, this has made Carlin one of the foremost experts on the history of the banjo and its playing styles. Bob has authored several instruction manuals and six DVDs on how to play clawhammer banjo. This has all combined to make Bob Carlin one of the most in-demand teachers at camps, workshops and festivals.

For Bob's books, recordings and more information about Bob, please go to *www.bobcarlinmusic.com*